Teaching Peace and War

This comprehensive volume on teaching peace and war demonstrates that our choice of pedagogy, or the way we structure a curriculum, must be attentive to context. Pedagogical strategies that work with one class may not work in another, whether over time or across space and different types of institutions, regardless of the field of study. This book offers insight on how to address these issues. The chapters contain valuable information on specific lessons learned and creative pedagogies developed, as well as exercises and tools that facilitate delivery in specific classrooms. The authors address a wide range of challenges related to broader questions on what teachers are trying to achieve when teaching about peace and war, including reflections on the teacher's role as a facilitator of knowledge creation.

This collection offers a valuable reference for scholars and instructors on structuring peace and war curricula in different global contexts and pedagogical strategies for a variety of classrooms.

The chapters in this book were originally published in the journal *Peace Review*.

Annick T.R. Wibben is Anna Lindh Professor for Gender, Peace and Security at the Swedish Defence University in Stockholm, Sweden. Her research straddles critical security and military studies, peace studies, and feminist international relations. She has written two books, *Feminist Security Studies: A Narrative Approach* (2011) and *Researching War: Feminist Methods, Ethics & Politics* (2016).

Amanda E. Donahoe is Assistant Professor of Political Science at Centenary College of Louisiana, USA. She teaches International Relations and Comparative Politics broadly, and the intersection of identity and peace/conflict processes more specifically. Her research focuses on gender and peacebuilding exemplified by her book *Peacebuilding through Women's Community Development: Wee Women's Work in Northern Ireland* (2017).

Teaching Peace and War
Pedagogy and Curricula

Edited by
Annick T.R. Wibben and
Amanda E. Donahoe

LONDON AND NEW YORK

First published 2020
by Routledge
2 Park Square, Milton Park, Abingdon, Oxon, OX14 4RN

and by Routledge
52 Vanderbilt Avenue, New York, NY 10017

Routledge is an imprint of the Taylor & Francis Group, an informa business

© 2020 Taylor & Francis

All rights reserved. No part of this book may be reprinted or reproduced
or utilised in any form or by any electronic, mechanical, or other means,
now known or hereafter invented, including photocopying and recording,
or in any information storage or retrieval system, without permission in
writing from the publishers.

Trademark notice: Product or corporate names may be trademarks or
registered trademarks, and are used only for identification and
explanation without intent to infringe.

British Library Cataloguing in Publication Data
A catalogue record for this book is available from the British Library

ISBN 13: 978-0-367-28027-7

Typeset in Times New Roman
by RefineCatch Limited, Bungay, Suffolk

Publisher's Note
The publisher accepts responsibility for any inconsistencies that may have
arisen during the conversion of this book from journal articles to book chapters,
namely the inclusion of journal terminology.

Disclaimer
Every effort has been made to contact copyright holders for their permission to
reprint material in this book. The publishers would be grateful to hear from any
copyright holder who is not here acknowledged and will undertake to rectify
any errors or omissions in future editions of this book.

Contents

Citation Information	vii
Notes on Contributors	xi

1. Peace and War in the Classroom   1
Amanda E. Donahoe and Annick T.R. Wibben

Part I: Pedagogy

2. Podcasting Pedagogy for Teaching Peace and War   6
Kujtese Bejtullahu, Rahel Kunz and Ruxandra Stoicescu

3. Teaching Peace with Popoki   14
Ronni Alexander

4. Teaching Peace Education at a South African University   22
Vaughn M. John

5. Participatory Action Research for Peacebuilding   31
Sylvia Kaye and Geoff Harris

6. Teaching Counterfactuals from Hell   38
Anjali Kaushlesh Dayal and Paul Musgrave

7. Truth, Sources, and the Fog of War   47
Joakim Berndtsson and Arne F. Wackenhut

8. Conflict and Engagement in "Reacting to the Past" Pedagogy   54
Julie C. Tatlock and Paula Reiter

9. Group Projects as Conflict Management Pedagogy   60
Amanda Ellsworth Donahoe

10. Teaching Religion, Conflict, and Peace   68
Tanya B. Schwarz

vi   CONTENTS

Part II: Curricula

11. Idealism Versus Pragmatism in Teaching Peace in Pakistan   74
    Zahid Shahab Ahmed

12. The Intrigue of Peace and War Curriculum in Africa   82
    Kudakwashe Chirambwi

13. Decolonizing Practices for Western Educators   92
    Michelle Rivera-Clonch

14. Teaching Peace, Not War, to U.S. History Students   101
    Timothy Braatz

15. War and Peace in Iraqi Kurdistan's History Curricula   110
    Marwan Darweish and Maamoon Alsayid Mohammed

16. Transrational Peacebuilding Education to Reduce Epistemic Violence   119
    Hilary Cremin, Josefina Echavarría and Kevin Kester

17. Teaching Tangible Peace   127
    Patrick T. Hiller

18. Teaching the United Nations, Gender, and Critical Pedagogy   133
    Georgina Holmes

19. Taking a Stand (or a Seat) in the Peace Studies Classroom   143
    Kyle B. T. Lambelet

20. Circle of Praxis Pedagogy for Peace Studies   150
    Mike Klein, Amy Finnegan and Jack Nelson-Pallmeyer

    Index   159

Citation Information

The following chapters were originally published in the journal *Peace Review*, volume 30, issues 1 and 3 (March/September 2018). When citing this material, please use the original page numbering for each article, as follows:

Chapter 2
Podcasting Pedagogy for Teaching Peace and War
Kujtese Bejtullahu, Rahel Kunz, and Ruxandra Stoicescu
Peace Review, volume 30, issue 1 (March 2018), pp. 1–8

Chapter 3
Teaching Peace with Popoki
Ronni Alexander
Peace Review, volume 30, issue 1 (March 2018), pp. 9–16

Chapter 4
Teaching Peace Education at a South African University
Vaughn M. John
Peace Review, volume 30, issue 1 (March 2018), pp. 53–61

Chapter 5
Participatory Action Research for Peacebuilding
Sylvia Kaye and Geoff Harris
Peace Review, volume 30, issue 1 (March 2018), pp. 62–68

Chapter 6
Teaching Counterfactuals from Hell
Anjali Kaushlesh Dayal and Paul Musgrave
Peace Review, volume 30, issue 1 (March 2018), pp. 23–31

Chapter 7
Truth, Sources, and the Fog of War
Joakim Berndtsson and Arne F. Wackenhut
Peace Review, volume 30, issue 1 (March 2018), pp. 32–38

Chapter 8
Conflict and Engagement in "Reacting to the Past" Pedagogy
Julie C. Tatlock and Paula Reiter
Peace Review, volume 30, issue 1 (March 2018), pp. 17–22

Chapter 9
Group Projects as Conflict Management Pedagogy
Amanda Ellsworth Donahoe
Peace Review, volume 30, issue 1 (March 2018), pp. 45–52

Chapter 10
Teaching Religion, Conflict, and Peace
Tanya B. Schwarz
Peace Review, volume 30, issue 1 (March 2018), pp. 39–44

Chapter 11
Idealism Versus Pragmatism in Teaching Peace in Pakistan
Zahid Shahab Ahmed
Peace Review, volume 30, issue 3 (September 2018), pp. 331–338

Chapter 12
The Intrigue of Peace and War Curriculum in Africa
Kudakwashe Chirambwi
Peace Review, volume 30, issue 3 (September 2018), pp. 312–321

Chapter 13
Decolonizing Practices for Western Educators
Michelle Rivera-Clonch
Peace Review, volume 30, issue 3 (September 2018), pp. 303–311

Chapter 14
Teaching Peace, Not War, to U.S. History Students
Timothy Braatz
Peace Review, volume 30, issue 3 (September 2018), pp. 339–347

Chapter 15
War and Peace in Iraqi Kurdistan's History Curricula
Marwan Darweish and Maamoon Alsayid Mohammed
Peace Review, volume 30, issue 3 (September 2018), pp. 322–330

Chapter 16
Transrational Peacebuilding Education to Reduce Epistemic Violence
Hilary Cremin, Josefina Echavarría and Kevin Kester
Peace Review, volume 30, issue 3 (September 2018), pp. 295–302

CITATION INFORMATION

Chapter 17
Teaching Tangible Peace
Patrick T. Hiller
Peace Review, volume 30, issue 3 (September 2018), pp. 279–284

Chapter 18
Teaching the United Nations, Gender, and Critical Pedagogy
Georgina Holmes
Peace Review, volume 30, issue 3 (September 2018), pp. 285–294

Chapter 19
Taking a Stand (or a Seat) in the Peace Studies Classroom
Kyle B. T. Lambelet
Peace Review, volume 30, issue 3 (September 2018), pp. 348–354

Chapter 20
Circle of Praxis Pedagogy for Peace Studies
Mike Klein, Amy Finnegan and Jack Nelson-Pallmeyer
Peace Review, volume 30, issue 3 (September 2018), pp. 270–278

For any permission-related enquiries please visit:
http://www.tandfonline.com/page/help/permissions

Notes on Contributors

Zahid Shahab Ahmed is a Research Fellow at Alfred Deakin Institute for Citizenship and Globalization at Deakin University, Australia. His teaching and research interests include diplomacy, foreign policy, and international organizations, with a special focus on South Asia.

Ronni Alexander is a Professor in the Kobe University Graduate School of International Cooperation Studies, Japan, and directs the university Gender Equality Office. She has been an activist for most of her life and began the Popoki Peace Project in 2006. She has lived in Japan since 1977.

Maamoon Alsayid Mohammed is a Lecturer in the Department of Peace and Human Rights at the University of Duhok, Kurdistan, Iraq. He is also a trainer in peace education and conflict transformation at the university's Centre for Peace and Conflict Resolution Studies.

Kujtese Bejtullahu resides in Geneva, where she completed her doctorate at the Graduate Institute of International and Development Studies, Switzerland. She enjoys teaching and writing about things that matter and things that don't.

Joakim Berndtsson is Associate Professor in Peace and Development Research and Assistant Head of the Department for Education at the School of Global Studies at the University of Gothenburg, Sweden. His research is mainly focused on different aspects of private security.

Timothy Braatz is a History Instructor, teaching history and nonviolence at Saddleback College, USA. He is also a novelist and playwright.

Kudakwashe Chirambwi is Programmes Officer at Peace in Action Trust, Zimbabwe. He is involved in developing peace education curricula in Africa. The primary focus of his research is on peace, security, and development in post-conflict Africa.

Hilary Cremin is a Reader at the Faculty of Education at the University of Cambridge, UK. She researches and teaches peacebuilding, in and through education, in settings in the United Kingdom and elsewhere. She has published her work extensively over a number of years.

NOTES ON CONTRIBUTORS

Marwan Darweish is Principal Lecturer in Peace Studies at the Centre for Trust, Peace and Social Relations at Coventry University, UK. His current research focuses on peace processes, conflict transformation, and nonviolence resistance.

Anjali Kaushlesh Dayal is Assistant Professor of International Politics at Fordham University, USA. She studies peace operations, peace processes, humanitarian intervention, and UN politics.

Amanda E. Donahoe is Assistant Professor of Political Science at Centenary College of Louisiana, USA. She teaches International Relations and Comparative Politics broadly, and the intersection of identity and peace/conflict processes more specifically. Her research focuses on gender and peacebuilding.

Josefina Echavarría is Senior Lecturer at the Unit for Peace and Conflict Studies at the University of Innsbruck, Austria. She works as facilitator, project consultant, and researcher on topics of (in)security, gender, peace and reconciliation, and migration.

Amy Finnegan is Assistant Professor and Chair of Justice and Peace Studies at the University of St. Thomas, USA. She is a sociologist, educator, researcher, and activist who is particularly keen on building spaces and opportunities for constructive dialogue across divergent perspectives.

Geoff Harris is a Professor in the International Centre of Nonviolence at Durban University of Technology, South Africa. His current research interests include restorative justice and demilitarization.

Patrick T. Hiller is the Executive Director of the War Prevention Initiative by the Jubitz Family Foundation and teaches Conflict Resolution at Portland State University, USA. He is Founding Editor of the *Peace Science Digest*.

Georgina Holmes is a Leverhulme Early Career Research Fellow in the Department of Politics and International Relations at the University of Reading, UK. Her research areas include gender, peacekeeping and security sector reform, and mediatized conflicts in the Great Lakes region of Africa.

Vaughn M. John works in the School of Education at the University of KwaZulu-Natal, South Africa. His teaching and research interests are in Peace Education, Adult Learning, and Research Methodology. He coordinates a Peace Education Programme.

Sylvia Kaye is a Senior Lecturer in the International Centre of Nonviolence at Durban University of Technology, South Africa. She researches the relationships between peace, development, and gender.

Kevin Kester is Assistant Professor of International Education and Global Affairs in the Department of Education at Keimyung University in Daegu, Korea. His research interests lie in the sociology and politics of education with a focus on the international system, social theory, peacebuilding, and qualitative research methods.

Mike Klein is an Assistant Professor in the Department of Justice and Peace Studies at the University of St. Thomas, USA. His research, writing, and consulting focus on democratizing leadership, peace education, intersections of art and social justice, and peacebuilding. He develops the agency with students and communities to transform social structures and advance social justice.

Rahel Kunz is a Senior Lecturer at the Institute of Political, Historical and International Studies at the University of Lausanne, Switzerland. Her research interests are feminist international political economy, gender issues in migration and development, gender and security sector reform, and feminist poststructuralist and postcolonial thought.

Kyle B. T. Lambelet is a Postdoctoral Fellow at Emory University's Candler School of Theology, USA. His teaching and research examine the role of religion and ethics in political violence and peacebuilding.

Paul Musgrave is Assistant Professor of Political Science at the University of Massachusetts–Amherst, USA. He studies U.S. foreign policy, oil politics, and the nature of international hierarchy.

Jack Nelson-Pallmeyer is Associate Professor of Justice and Peace Studies at the University of St. Thomas, USA. He is an activist academic whose life and work are focused on addressing the political, economic, faith, and foreign policy dimensions of hunger and poverty.

Paula Reiter is Associate Professor of English at Mount Mary University, USA. She teaches British literature, composition, and linguistics.

Michelle Rivera-Clonch is Assistant Professor of Psychology at Antioch College, USA. She is an educator, therapist, consultant, and researcher in the fields of psychology, counseling, peace studies, and grassroots leadership models.

Tanya B. Schwarz is Associate Director of Academic and Professional Development at the American Political Science Association, USA. Her work examines the role of religion in peace, conflict, and global governance.

Ruxandra Stoicescu is an independent researcher and media producer based in Geneva, Switzerland. She loves radio and literature and seeks to bring them ever closer to the study of international relations.

Julie C. Tatlock is Assistant Professor of History, and Chair of the Department of Justice, Sociology, and History at Mount Mary University, USA. She specializes in world history and European history.

Arne F. Wackenhut is Adjunct Lecturer in Global Studies at the School of Global Studies at the University of Gothenburg, Sweden. He is particularly interested in questions relating to grassroots mobilization for socio-political change in less-democratic settings.

Annick T.R. Wibben is Anna Lindh Professor for Gender, Peace and Security at the Swedish Defence University in Stockholm, Sweden. Her research straddles critical security and military studies, peace studies, and feminist international relations.

Peace and War in the Classroom

AMANDA E. DONAHOE AND ANNICK T.R. WIBBEN

"If the purpose of teaching about war is to understand the past in order to prevent repetition in the future, the purpose of teaching peace is to create that future"

These are the words of Ronni Alexander whose essay, part of a pair of *Peace Review* special issues on Teaching Peace and War, is also included here. When we put out the call for submissions to a special issue of *Peace Review* on teaching about peace and war in summer 2017, we never dreamed of receiving 70 essays. As scholars deeply concerned with pedagogy, we were excited to receive them—clearly the topic hit a nerve. Consequently, we were lucky enough to be able to edit not one, but two special issues on teaching and curricular issues: Volume 30, issue 1 (January–March 2018) and Volume 30, issue 3 (July–September 2018). This book represents the collection of essays from both issues.

Across the essays in these two special issues a key theme emerged: Teaching peace and war, whether in choice of pedagogy or in structuring a curriculum, must be attentive to context. This seems obvious, perhaps. Teaching is always contextual. Pedagogical strategies that work with one class may not in another, whether over time or across space and different types of institutions, regardless of the field of study. The essays collected here make this abundantly clear, but they also offer much insight on how to address small and large issues. When you peruse these essays, you will find much valuable information on specific lessons learned, and creative pedagogies developed, as well as exercises and tools created that facilitate delivery in our specific classrooms. At the same time, you will see scholars grappling with a wide range of challenges related to broader questions on what it is we are trying to achieve when teaching about peace and war, including reflections on the teacher's role as a facilitator of knowledge creation.

Those of us who teach about peace and war do so from a variety of perspectives—as scholars and practitioners we draw on a wide range of global frames and academic disciplines, some more concerned with understanding (and even developing strategies for) war, others steeped in efforts to build and maintain peace. While many of the contributors to this collection broadly identify with peace and conflict studies (itself a varied and interdisciplinary field as it draws on political science, history, geography, sociology, and education among others), we have also tried to include others who have important contributions to make, specifically outside of the Anglo-American context which tends to dominate in this field. While it can be a challenge to teach about peace and war without a unified body of foundational literature to draw on, we believe that this is also a strength if we commit to a purposeful awareness and expectation of inclusivity, both theoretically in terms of these varied fields of study and methodologically as a counter to various kinds of exclusion that often drive conflict.

The organization of the book largely follows that of the special issues. Part I is on pedagogy and focuses specifically on classroom strategies but also asks us to consider some broader themes applicable beyond the teaching of peace and war: Do you present knowledge as settled or up for debate? Do you engage students in the construction of knowledge, maybe emphasizing their local/indigenous knowledges and prior experiences? How might a teacher use practical exercises and new technologies in class and creatively engage materials to defamiliarize accepted wisdom and inspire new insights? Each essay in this collection is a treasure-trove of knowledge—some specifically develop new assignments, others make creative use of new technologies, yet others emphasize experiential knowledge and links to activism.

Part I starts with Bejtullahu, Kunz & Stoicescu's essay on podcasting which argues that such a creative assignment encourages students to develop a "more attentive examination of [the class'] content and the development of academic responsibility toward it" and Alexander's description of the ways in which the fictional character Popoki can help inspire deeper thinking about what peace means by "incorporating art-making and the use of our senses, emotions, and bodies along with our intellect". In day-long sessions for part-time students in South Africa, John flips the classroom in a multi-stage conflict mapping project that engages students in a collaborative classroom environment. Kaye & Harris reach beyond the academic world in their adoption of (participatory) action research in working with doctoral students across the African continent. Like Alexander, Kaye & Harris emphasize the "community as participants and direct beneficiaries", noting that this allows newly created knowledge to be directly relevant to communities and, hopefully, to promote more immediate change than traditional academic research.

In their essay, Dayal & Musgrave take on the idea that we can teach specific "lessons of history" and suggest we might instead focus on "guiding students to the recognition that some questions are unanswerable". They suggest that a focus on counterfactuals, uncertainty and unintended consequences, while also specifically addressing students' ethical concerns, better serves to convey the complexity, e.g. of decisions to intervene (or not). Berndtsson & Wackenhut offer another approach to the challenge of teaching emotionally and ethically different knowledge about violence/war: Using the

My Lai massacre as their case, they develop a comprehensive exercise that involves original documents with conflicting accounts that the students are asked to analyze, research further and eventually present. In the process of participating in the exercise, the students not only learn key skills, the exercise also underlines "the difficulties of arriving at a single and 'true' narrative" of any event.

Finally, Tatlock & Reiter use extensive role play to teach historical knowledge and, at the same time, help students hone key skills such as empathy, critical listening, and argumentation. Similarly, Donahoe makes creative use of group work to not just teach about conflict resolution, but to apply conflict management techniques in the group activities themselves. Schwarz, meanwhile, encourages students to reflect on their preconceived notions of the relationship between religion and politics in general as well as of religious traditions as monolithic and unchanging. Each of these essays emphasizes the importance of teaching students reflexivity—both teachers and scholars need to become aware of prejudgements we bring to a particular topic and acknowledge our varied positionality as Wibben has elsewhere noted.

Part II focuses on peace and war (studies) curricula. It starts by drawing attention to standards of import and how they continue to change. This discussion is followed by contributions that focus on the tension between curriculum standards and bottom-up contextual teaching. Whether in Iraqi Kurdistan, Pakistan, various African cases or even the United Nations universities, the authors wrestle with the difficulties of addressing local needs and contexts when faced with established scholarship that is often received as a Western imposition. This problem of translating global standards in the implementation of curricula presents an opportunity to critically engage the intersection of global and local—whose perspective should be prioritized? To what end? The final set of essays consider the ways in which attention to, as well as an explicit embrace of, positionality in the classroom can contribute positively to the normative endeavor of teaching peace and war. In addition to offering critical assessments, many of the essays in these pages offer practical applications and innovative ways forward.

There are varied lessons to be learned in the experiences our colleagues share: Practically applying the ideal of inclusion is a key challenge in the field. For example, as Ahmed discusses, Pakistan's education system is characterized by a three-tier educational system in which a one-size-fits-all approach to teaching peace cannot succeed. Chirambwi is similarly critical of ready-made frameworks for teaching peace in various African states where high dropout rates and increasing levels of student-trauma present specific challenges to education broadly and peace education directly, especially as it is delivered by soldiers as peace educators. Finnegan et al. suggest that inserting or immersing students into the experiences of marginalized people can help ground students in contextual learning. Teaching peace and war, as Rivera-Clonch argues, should be both systemic and contextual, empowering local knowledges and drawing on local wisdom. In the classroom we can draw on both the diversity of the students' knowledges and on our own experiences to contribute to these processes.

Critical thinking is imperative to the learning process, particularly as Braatz points out, when students are often taught war-worship, as Wibben et al. note in their recent reflection on Feminist Peace Research. Instead, students should be encouraged to question whether something is true; how we know it is true; why the story is important; and what and where the silences are. Darweish & Mohammed, Cremin, Echavarría & Kester, and Braatz are all particularly concerned with the issue of nationalism and the ways in which national narratives go unchallenged. Critical pedagogies are a necessary process in deconstructing the myths that promote the status quo. Hiller suggests that two particularly destructive and dominant myths in this field are that violent conflict is natural and that peace is weakness and naivete. At the same time, recognizing the limitations and weaknesses of various peace processes is an important component of critical pedagogy. As Holmes addresses, such pedagogy disrupts repressive knowledge claims in the classroom—she and others acknowledge Paolo Freire as foundational to teaching this field.

A final motif is teacher subjectivity. Teaching peace and war is inherently a normative endeavor. Chirambwi argues that "the content of peace education reflects positionality, crystallization and solidification of political affiliation". We cannot help but bring our own norms into the classroom whether, as Lambelet discusses, we stand up and take responsibility for our own commitments or sit down and facilitate our students taking responsibility for theirs. Recognizing that we (students and teachers) arrive in the classroom with prior experience and varied training and that we work within the limits of particular contexts, if acknowledged and specifically addressed should be considered a strength rather than a weakness because it makes us better teachers (and scholars).

In the final essay of this collection, Klein, Finnegan & Nelson-Pallmeyer promote a Circle of Praxis pedagogy; a purposeful and iterative process of insertion, descriptive analysis, normative analysis and action planning. This call to conscientious structure both within the classroom and across the curriculum promotes transformative education. Like the other essays in this collection, theirs offers a great deal of practical wisdom from colleagues in a variety of fields and a variety of spaces under the umbrella of peace and conflict studies.

We should also note that the essays in this volume represent less than a third of the collection of essays that were submitted to this project; our colleagues are truly doing amazing work. As we see it, these essays offer an invitation to engage in an ongoing conversation about the ways in which we can teach and facilitate learning in our classrooms. This project has been particularly rewarding for us—we have enjoyed learning from the essays here and the wider pool of essays submitted in response to our call. We have learned specific strategies that we are already implementing in our classrooms and much more that we look forward to applying in the future. We hope that you will find these essays similarly challenging and inspiring.

REFERENCES

Wibben, Annick T.R. (Ed.) 2016. *Researching War: Feminist Methods, Ethics & Politics.* London & New York: Routledge.

Wibben, Annick T.R., Catia Confortini, Sarai Aharoni, Sanam Roohi, Leena Vastapuu & Tiina Vaittinen. 2018. Collective Discussion: Piecing-Up Feminist Peace Research. *International Political Sociology.* doi: 10.1093/ips/oly034

Podcasting Pedagogy for Teaching Peace and War

KUJTESE BEJTULLAHU, RAHEL KUNZ AND RUXANDRA STOICESCU

Audio podcasting is a powerful way of communicating in today's world. Radio and audio podcasts are used in conflict situations, both as a tool for instigating and preventing it, or building peace. Radio stations, such as those set up by the Hirondelle Foundation, have been established specifically in conflict settings to get parties to dialogue, to diffuse unsubstantiated rumors, and to provide more "balanced" reporting of news.

Podcasts have already become a pedagogical tool in the social sciences, but less so in International Relations (IR). There is an ongoing debate about the pedagogical risks and benefits of using podcasts in the classroom, but the literature does not explore how different disciplines can engage with the medium. When podcasts are predominantly used as a source of information or a way of disseminating it, one can question their pedagogical usefulness depending on content and receptivity, as Steven Lonn and Stephanie Teasley do. If, however, one shifts attention from podcasts as finished products to podcasting as a process of putting together and narrating stories, then it is this collaborative *mise-en-scène* and the creative choices and affects that go with it that matter pedagogically.

Through the lens of writings on using podcasts in higher education and on critical/alternative pedagogy in IR, we explore—in the following—the potential for podcasting in teaching peace and war. We draw on our experience of co-teaching a course on International Security using podcasting in an interactive process of teaching, learning, and evaluation. By designing and producing their own podcast, students not only used them as a source of information, but experienced podcasting as a more creative and reflective process of exploring and narrating challenging stories about peace and war.

We argue that podcasting is particularly suited to the study of peace and war because it encourages students to relay facts and arguments, and to include the different sensibilities that render some arguments or narratives more believable and memorable than others. Podcasting encourages students to fine-tune their listening skills; to think about creative ways to voice difficult problems and conversations to a concerned audience; and to scrutinize the "scriptedness" behind existing stories on peace and war. Ultimately, we propose that the pedagogical potential of podcasting is its ability to embody and humanize the study of peace and war in a way that traditional IR teaching struggles to do.

The literature on the use of podcasts in higher education ranges from extolling its virtues to doubting its efficacy in helping students improve their academic performance. New technologies do not necessarily open up our thinking. While the use of podcasting with other social goals remains something to develop or debate, certain studies show that they can bring strong learning benefits when students engage in their production. Specifically, the responsibility of delivering a product encourages a more attentive examination of its content and the development of academic responsibility toward it. Key advantages include ease of production, portability, synthetic presentation of a subject, as well as experimenting with language, format, and target audience.

O ur starting point was that a mix of creative freedom, technical training, varied sources, and reflective probing can not only turn podcasting into a memorable and stimulating learning experience for students, but it can also help embody and humanize the study of peace and war. Therefore, we linked up with the literature on critical/alternative pedagogies in IR where authors cite the use of alternative tools and sites for teaching and learning. Naeem Inayatullah uses Music of the African Diaspora to develop student's aesthetic and political sensibilities. Felix Rösch teaches IR through contact improvisation dance. Shiera El-Malik proposes various "experiments in intimacy" in the classroom in an attempt to "expose, and potentially disrupt, contemporary knowledge practices" and to "unseat practices that yield to processes of 'thingification.'" The search for critical/alternative pedagogies reflects a more profound desire to decolonize or displace existing logics that are familiar, but painfully so. As Henry Giroux underlines, one of the key elements of critical learning is to "unsettle common sense, make power accountable, and connect classroom knowledge to larger civic issues."

The literature on the so-called aesthetic turn further strengthens the case for podcasting. It highlights the limits of more traditional IR scholarship, which privileges logical reasoning, but struggles to accommodate situations or conversations that are difficult because they do not quite conform to expected logics. We need to allow for the possibility, too, that in-your-face questions of (in)security cannot always be contained in neat matrices or the logical expectations we draw around them, for they also involve an interplay of emotions and aesthetics, at times a certain "excess" that we cannot quite pin down but cannot ignore either. To talk about peace and war more meaningfully, we must bring forth a wider palette of emotions and the sensibilities around them that make some voices resonate more than others. Yet these are not easily taught nor acquired. As Roland Bleiker points out, this requires us to mobilize a wider register of human faculties, moving "back and forth between imagination and reason, thought and sensibility, memory and understanding, without imposing one faculty upon another."

In designing our course, we engaged with the idea that it is pedagogically and politically important to encourage an interplay of various sensibilities in the classroom so as to carve our way to insights that help us talk about uncomfortable, vexing, sometimes irresolvable aspects of international politics, such as the experience of war, the cost of peace, or how security turns on itself. Interlacing the literature on podcasting, critical security studies, and the aesthetic turn in IR, we further explored how podcasting can help us move away from the traditional "scriptedness" of the discipline so as to tune in to other possibilities—of listening, voice, and embodiment—when broaching questions of peace and war. How, more pragmatically, can podcasting help students navigate that challenging nexus where the political invests us intellectually, emotionally, and aesthetically too? We now present some insights from our experience, which may be applicable to other courses on peace and war or in IR more broadly.

Our course was structured around four types of activities: introductory lectures on peace, war, and security; reading and debating sessions on more specific themes—such as securitization, gender and (in)security, terrorism and security, privatization of security, security and migration, the quotidian and (in)security; workshop modules on listening and developing a voice, multimedia analysis, the technicalities of producing a scenario, recording and editing a podcast; and presentations by external experts working in the field of radio and podcast production. It also included a number of sessions on peer and teacher feedback to ensure a more interactive and reflexive learning experience.

While the basic parameters of podcast production were specified in a guide, there was substantial freedom in the choice of subject, style of expression, the types of sources or testimonies brought in, the choice of tone, sound design, the overall *mise-en-scène*, and the different creative elements behind it. In the process of conceptualizing and producing their podcast, students autonomously acquired theoretical and empirical knowledge relevant to their topic. We encouraged a creative play with sources by combining scientific articles and newspaper material with podcasts, narratives, historic testimonials, rituals from the quotidian, poetry, curated imagery, videos, talks, and so forth.

To talk about the experience of peace and war, we brought into conversation the academic with the poetic, such as present in Carol Nordstrom's piece *A Different Kind of War Story*. Exploring securitization theory, we discussed not only its enabling conditions or why certain issues are easier to "securitize" than others, but what the ritualized incantation of a charged phrase like weapons of mass destruction (WMD) does to public debate and understanding of security. Talking about terrorism, we reflected, with Judith Butler's voice, on how the experience of terror laces the personal with the political, and on the difficulty of bearing our grief and others' loss without wielding further destruction. We reflected, too, on whether talking more about bearing loss can help us live with our fears, or when to question how much security is enough.

Students were invited to probe the limits of what constitutes "proper" academic practice, and to question what we should be mindful about when it comes to narrating the experience of violence or its political significance. Why do we read some points of view or listen to some voices more than others? Why do we find certain sources more credible or relevant and others more forgettable or negligible? Given the above, students had to think about what kind of sources, voices, testimonies, or experiences to bring into their podcasts, why and how.

This process of meeting in groups to flesh out the meaningful sources or testimonies, the choice of words, music, or location for recording together with the actual recording, enacting, and editing of living voices also introduced an embodied effort. A key criticism leveled at traditional IR pedagogy is the way in which it renders the study of peace and war abstract and disembodied. Scholars such as Shiera El-Malik, Himadeep Muppidi, and Erzsebet Strausz approach this from different angles, pointing to a common trend, equally verified by us: increasingly in undergraduate courses, students receive their reading pack in an online folder, with little incentive to visit a library or archive, conduct interviews, collect different testimonies, or look for the concrete ways in which abstract questions of peace and war, or international politics more broadly, are manifest in people's lives. Encouraging a more creative play with sources whereby students had to make their bodies move as much as their voices and brains allowed them to embody academic activity. This process helps withstand that tendency to turn students into passive absorbers of knowledge who often end up feeling distanced.

Podcasting is also promising because it contributes to humanizing the study of peace and war. Students often already share their political views or frustrations through social media, but using a podcast in class challenges them to elaborate on complex problems and academic concepts in a way that can resonate with a broader audience, themselves included. As such, podcasting encourages students to invest themselves as students, teachers, and concerned members of society at once. They actively search for the sounds and utterances that make it possible to translate a complex problem of peace and war into a shared concern. They must work, too, with that challenge of striking too distant or abstract a note that obscures the human in their story. The way in which podcasting fosters student attentiveness to human voices, choices, limits, emotions, misunderstandings, hopes, missed expectations, and so forth, is by encouraging them to revisit and practice the ways in which political grievances and problems can be expressed. Namely, it helps them become better attuned to the importance of listening, voicing, and ways of un/re-scripting the difficult, at times ambiguous, conversations that are part and parcel of debates on peace and war.

To emphasize the power and ethics of listening, we explored in class not only how to be attentive to subtler aspects of utterances or sounds—including the use of tone, silences, irony, humor, repetitive chants, and so on—but also to the responsibilities that come with listening. We discussed Italo Calvino's *Un roi à l'écoute*, a text that reveals a sovereign who tends to his power through intense listening of everything that might be happening in corners of his palace, behind the curtains, in whispers, sighs, movements, silences, laughs, and so on. Through such heightened surveillance, he dissolves his presence in a network of ears and echoes, sometimes hearing his own doubts loudest. The point about listening is not only that it may be useful or necessary; it matters too how and to whom we listen when we cannot listen to everything at the same time nor listen to ourselves only.

P articularly interesting was the experience of students listening to their own podcasts during and at the end of the course: how they sounded to themselves and their audience when role-playing experts, politicians, concerned citizens, migrants, or victims; when stereotyping or caricaturing them too; when assigning gendered roles to their voices; when reproducing too much of the same trope or clarifying one "-ism" by way of another. Also fascinating was how they varied the tones or used background noises, pauses, irony, humor, sighs of frustration, interruptions, escalation of voices or meditative sounds to dramatize, stimulate, or subdue the audience into thinking or feeling. This listening to how we sound when tackling questions of peace and war made possible further reflection that beyond the desire to sound appealing, there is also a certain responsibility to engage a public in a meaningful way.

Central to podcasting on peace and war is also the question of voice, or voicing as an active but selective way of broaching something that is difficult to do. Students not only had to make choices which voices to include but also how: how loud, serious, ridiculous, articulate, distant, moving, and so forth. They had to think moreover about where or what was their voice in that noise they produced. One of the interesting things was that unlike an academic paper that often lays its premises to deliver its punch line,

TEACHING PEACE AND WAR

some of the podcasts treated a problem or debate without resolving it. This reveals a unique potential of podcasting: working in a group, different voices appear; the differences or multiplicities present are not easily or necessarily dissolved; students allow themselves to experience some discomfort before proposing a quick fix. They explore, instead, how to voice something and how to perceive the *mise-en-scène* of different voices, including our own, in a debate.

Finally, podcasting also helps students reflect on working with scripts and the "scriptedness" of politics. As they developed their concept, students moved between drafting a script and enacting it. Printed in black and white, words still keep their nuances, but sounds also have their way: silencing us into reflection, tuning us in, making our bodies move. As the students toyed with both words and sounds to produce something resonant, they discovered the challenge of realizing a *mise-en-scène* that was somewhat scripted, but not unduly, or overly so. Pedagogically speaking, the students had to make that quasi-paradoxical move where they include the familiar scripts in their heads and books and how much those needed tweaking: what to unscript? Where to rescript? Thus discussing what scripts do for and to us in international politics, we touched in particular on binary-driven thinking that all too often hands us scripts to follow without beckoning reflection. The discipline of IR, and debates on security, are particularly susceptible to binary set ups, such as between realism or idealism, enemy and friend, North and South, state and nonstate actors, axis of good and evil, international saviors and victims, rational and irrational actors, and so on. This is one of the most valuable but challenging pedagogical points to communicate: how do we un-script ourselves out of binaries we no longer believe to be taking us anywhere meaningful? How do we strike a different note that permits us an insight or perhaps a question we might not habitually ask? What if peace is not an acquiescent state? Then what is war? And what would happen if our discourse did not split them always so?

Through podcasting, we can un/rescript pedagogy for teaching peace and war in a number of ways. Paying attention to various genres and taking seriously humor and poetry, practicing listening and voicing skills, and dehumanizing and embodying the study of peace and war, students' multiple sensibilities are fine-tuned. This opens up alternative ways of experiencing the study of peace and war. In Strausz's words: as "autonomous thinking and feeling beings who turn(ed) to the other with compassion and care." It allows us to inhabit the space of international relations as a site of connection, respect, and shared understanding. It also encourages to move beyond black and white thinking, even to question the idea that there is a clear difference between peace and war, or that we must study them by distancing one from the other.

ACKNOWLEDGMENT

This essay grew out of a course on *International Security* co-taught by the three authors in 2016 in the context of a teaching innovation project.

FUNDING

Funding by the Pedagogic Innovation Fund of the Université de Lausanne is gratefully acknowledged.

RECOMMENDED READINGS

Bleiker, Roland. 2001. "The Aesthetic Turn in International Political Theory." *Millennium: Journal of International Studies* 30 (3). doi:10.1177/03058298010300031001.

Bleiker, Roland and Emma Hutchison. 2008. "Fear No More: Emotions and World Politics." *Review of International Studies* 34. doi:10.1017/S0260210508007821.

Butler, Judith. 2014. *Speaking of Rage and Grief*. 10th Annual PEN World Voices Festival of International Literature. Available at <https://www.youtube.com/watch?v=ZxyabzopQi8>, last accessed January 8, 2018.

Calvino, Italo. 1990. *Un roi à l'écoute*. Paris: Gallimard.

Cann, Alan J. 2007. "Podcasting is Dead. Long Live Video!" *Bioscience Education Journal* 10 (1): 1–4.

El-Malik, Shiera S. 2013. "Critical Pedagogy as Interrupting Thingification." *Critical Studies on Security* 1 (3). doi:10.1080/21624887.2013.850230.

Fernandez, Vicenc, Pep Simo, and Jose M. Sallan. 2009. "Podcasting: A New Technological Tool to Facilitate Good Practice in Higher Education." *Computers and Education* 53. doi:10.1016/j.compedu.2009.02.014.

Giroux, Henry. 2014. *Neoliberalism's War on Higher Education*. Chicago: Haymarket Books.

Inayatullah, Naeem. 2013. "Playing on the Shores of an Imperial Pedagogy." *Critical Studies on Security* 1 (3). doi:10.1080/21624887.2013.850225.

Lazzari, Marco. 2009. "Creative use of Podcasting in Higher Education and its Effect on Competitive Agency." *Computers and Education* 51 (2): 27–34.

Lonn, Steven and Teasley Stephanie. 2009. "Podcasting in Higher Education: What are the Implications for Teaching and Learning?" *Internet and Higher Education* 12. doi:10.1016/j.iheduc.2009.06.002.

Mishra, Pankaj. 2016. "Welcome to the Age of Anger." *The Guardian*. Available at <https://www.theguardian.com/politics/2016/dec/08/welcome-age-anger-brexit-trump>, last accessed November 27, 2017.

Muppidi, Himadeep. 2012. *The Colonial Signs of International Relations*. New York: Columbia University Press.

Nordstrom, Carol. 1997. *A Different Kind of War Story*. Philadelphia: University of Pennsylvania Press.

Oren, Ido and Ty Solomon. 2015. "WMD, WMD, WMD: Securitisation through Ritualised Incantation of Ambiguous Phrases." *Review of International Studies* 4 (1/2): 313–336.

Picq, Lavinas. 2013. "Critics at the Edge? Decolonizing Methodologies in International Relations." *International Political Science Review* 34 (4). doi:10.1177/0192512113493224.

Rösch, Felix. 2017. "The Power of Dance: Teaching International Relations Through Contact Improvisation." *International Studies Perspectives*. doi:10.1093/isp/ekx002.

Strausz, Erzsebet. Forthcoming 2018. "International Pedagogical Relations in Fragments: Politics and Poetics in the Classroom and Beyond," in Andreas Gofas, Inanna Hamati-Ataya, and Nicholas Onuf (eds.), *The SAGE Handbook of the History, Philosophy and Sociology of International Relations*. London: SAGE.

Teaching Peace with Popoki

RONNI ALEXANDER

If the purpose of teaching about war is to understand the past in order to prevent repetition in the future, the purpose of teaching peace is to create that future. While many of us may live in places that are not currently at war or where the horrific consequences of war are not readily visible, no one anywhere lives in a place that is completely free of violence, direct or otherwise. Understanding peace to include the absence of not only war but also violence and avoidable harm, even those living far from armed conflict are not living completely in peace. To teach peace is therefore to challenge our students and ourselves to imagine something that none us has experienced.

The following will introduce some of the peace education praxis of the Popoki Peace Project, a grassroots initiative that I began in 2006 in Japan focusing on peace learning, teaching, and activism. Most of the work of the Project takes place outside of the regular curriculum and/or classroom, generally taking the form of workshops of varying lengths (somewhere between 90 minutes and several days), but the activities and thinking from these programs have found their way into all of my teaching. The purpose of this essay is not to offer a curriculum for the teaching of peace, but rather, to offer ways that the teaching of peace can be enriched by incorporating art-making and the use of our senses, emotions, and bodies along with our intellect. Beginning with a short description of the Popoki Peace Project, I will then introduce some activities that might be useful to educators working with students of all ages and backgrounds.

Popoki, a cat with a rainbow tail, is the symbol and energy behind the Popoki Peace Project. It was originally established to publish and use in my first picture book, *Popoki, What Color is Peace?* In the first half of that book, Popoki helps to ask questions about the color, taste, smell, feel, and sound of peace. In the second half, questions are based on situations from his life: is peace being able to object strenuously to something you don't like? Is your peace related to that of others? Is peace being able to go to school?, and

---

Color versions of one or more of the figures in the article can be found online at www.tandfonline.com/cper.

so on. These questions are not answered in the text. Instead, the reader is left to find her/his own responses and to raise new questions. The Popoki Peace Project uses questions from Popoki's books in conjunction with creative projects and movements in teaching peace.

The work of the Popoki Peace Project and the activities introduced here are based on several premises about ways of knowing and expression. The first is that since we first encounter and know the world through our bodies, our bodily experience plays an important role in what we know and how we know it, even though many intellectual traditions do not recognize that knowledge as legitimate. The second is that imagination and creativity are firmly linked to experience, particularly in adults. Peace is an extremely abstract and complex concept. Negative peace—no war, no human rights violations, and so on—is far easier to imagine and work toward than positive peace, something that is more than the sum of its negative parts. Negative peace is an important step on the journey to Popoki's ultimate goal of positive peace.

The third premise is that stories are important and that there is never just one story or only one way to tell it. Peace, too, has multiple versions and stories. One of our objectives is to identify those stories and find ways to navigate among them. This view challenges binary understandings of social relations and seeks inclusion, welcoming difference as a potential source for creative change.

The fourth premise is that while words are extremely useful and important, there are many things that people do not, or cannot, express in words. In some cases the overwhelming power of particular oral and/or written discourses prevents alternative voices from being heard. In other cases, there may not be words for what is being expressed. Popoki uses art-making as an opportunity to explore the potential of alternative modes of expression for sharing ideas that are not verbalized and for discovering new dimensions of our own thinking and being.

The Popoki Peace Project emphasizes bodies, stories, and art-making in activities that generally have a theme or focus such as peace or human rights. We understand that violence often has invisible beginnings, so that for, example, war does not begin when the first shots are fired, nor does it end when the ceasefire goes into effect. We try to help students to see these less visible aspects of violence, particularly processes of militarization, racism, and gendered social relations, issues that can be sensitive and controversial. We try to ensure that our teaching environments are peaceful, inclusive, and feel safe, and to conclude all lessons with activities to help students to imagine new and different worlds, and to find their own places in them.

Peace and security are deeply intertwined. Popoki understands security to mean both the physicality of being safe but also the feeling of being safe. These aspects are generally understood to be overlapping, but in fact, often the subjectivity of feeling safe is ignored. This has been made very clear to us by the Popoki Friendship Story project, work begun shortly after the March 2011 earthquake, tsunami, and nuclear meltdowns in northeastern Japan. Shortly after the disaster, I began a project in the affected area that involved inviting evacuees and others to draw freely on a long (500 cm × 45 cm) cloth stretched on the floor, or any available space. Many people, young and old, came to draw and when they did, they shared their stories and began to interact with one another. Some become friends. Initially intended to last a month or two, the project is in its sixth year. Most of the early drawings on the cloths represented stories of grief, fear, anger, and confusion. More recently, people share their stories and feelings of being unsafe, even when they are told otherwise, as in the case of the man who said a new, 14.5 meter sea wall is said to be for the safety of his community, but it will not make him feel safe because it will prevent him from being able to see any changes in the ocean. The experience with this project has convinced me of the importance of feelings of being safe, and has underscored for me the power of art-making as a mode of expression. This conviction is reflected in the teaching activities introduced below, a few of the many ways to explore peace with Popoki.

M y understanding of pedagogy is that regardless of the content, position-ing and framing helps learners to focus on the material and understand what might be expected of them. For learning activities that require group work, it is useful to have a feeling of unity established before those activi-ties begin. Of course, it is also nice to have relaxed, focused students. This is a long-winded way of saying that when doing this work, warming up is necessary, even for groups that frequently work together.

Popoki's easiest method of getting a group ready to learn is "Poga", each monthly issue of Popoki News has a Poga section, but there are no particular rules (see the Archives at http://popoki.cruisejapan.com). Poga is done as a group, and is led by a facilitator (not necessarily the teacher) and consists of a few minutes of stretches or easy exercises geared to the abilities of the group. Generally we begin with sitting up straight and quietly, and end with a success (I did it!) pose. If possible, some sort of physical interaction is useful because it always makes people smile, even if it is a smile of embarrassment.

Poga changes the flow of air in the room, refreshes and relaxes the partic-ipants, and sets the stage for further interaction. It is in many ways a simple conflict prevention and/or resolution tool. Poga is playful and unlike yoga, there are no rules. It is not competitive and should not be offered in such a way as to make some people feel they are not good at it. Instead, Poga can be a chance for everyone to laugh at themselves and their mistakes. For Popoki, bodies and sensations are important, and even simple exercises help learners to develop an awareness of their bodies, the space around them, and the connection between their bodies and their minds. Once people are familiar with Poga, it is also helpful at those moments in the classroom where tensions have risen, the atmosphere has become too intense or the air has become stale.

Lessons with Popoki frequently include reading of a few pages from one or more Popoki Peace Books. I also often draw on techniques from such work as *Theatre of the Oppressed*, by Augusto Boal, or Playback Theatre, asking students to make statues or tableaux with their bodies and other activities to physically express the key concepts of the lesson. Whenever possible, intellectual activity is combined with movement. For example, rather than handing students a list of words related to peace and asking them to discuss and/or rank them, Popoki gives them sets of word cards and asks them to *arrange* them in a way that shows their importance/relation to peace. Most students understand this to mean that the cards should be arranged in a single line. Helping them to make different configurations sets the stage for discussions of the complexity of the concept itself, as well as showing how students have different understandings of concepts such as law or justice, and/or relationships among those concepts that are often taken for granted or left unchallenged. As part of this exercise, I often ask students to choose one word from their collection and use their bodies collectively to make a statue that represents its meaning.

D rawing is a very important part of Popoki's work because, as mentioned above, what is expressed by people when they draw is often different from what they convey when they speak or write. Regardless of whether it is articulated by the artist, or s/he is conscious of the details, every drawing has a story. Popoki's drawing activities can be divided into those that focus on drawing without asking specifically for a story and those that involve story-making as well as drawing.

Most of Popoki's activities that focus on drawing are group activities. These activities can be part of a lesson with specific age groups or classes, but can just as easily be part of a workshop program involving people of all ages, from the very young to the very old. After engaging in preparatory activities such as those outlined above, groups are given a large paper and colored markers and/or crayons and asked to draw. These drawings usually have a theme such as a "peace garden where you can walk or play with Popoki," or "a peaceful town where you can live with Popoki," or "a place where you and Popoki can feel safe." All of the drawings must include Popoki, be peaceful for all genders, and include sensory expressions. When the drawings are completed they can be shared and discussed.

These drawings generally represent some image of positive peace, sometimes showing the transformation of conflict and/or issues addressed earlier in the class or workshop. Sometimes groups are asked to include a conflict, either at the beginning or during the process. This can help them to think about conflict resolution or conflict prevention in the context of their drawing. Often groups do not include themselves in the drawings, so asking them how it would be different, or what they would be doing if they were there can help them to develop their understanding of why (or if) their drawing represents peace rather than, for example, happiness.

Sometimes drawing activities are done individually and do not necessarily involve Popoki. For example, students can be asked to draw the smell of feeling safe. Just this simple assignment can lead to a discussion on the complexities of feeling safe and differences among the students. One such discussion with a group of graduate students in the United States revealed a huge difference in the level of safety students felt in that particular classroom and led to a discussion not only about how to make them feel safer but about the relationship between feeling safe and peace.

Another example comes from a seminar on gender I give for government officials from developing countries who are in Japan for training. I usually begin by asking them to draw a picture of "gender equality." When they are finished, we discuss the difference between what they have drawn and what they talk about in their offices when they address gender equality. Most of the time, the drawings and office realities are very different. This opens up space for the interrogation of individual and social differences, including critical discussion of issues such as the public/private divide or gender diversity. These are uncomfortable topics for many of the participants, and the use of drawing and stories generally makes them a bit more willing to engage in discussion.

A particularly useful tool that involves individual work and uses drawing and story-making is to tell students that Popoki has met a soldier, terrorist, and so on and ask them to draw and describe the person in detail. We then share the drawings and stories. This is a good introductory activity because in the space of a very short time it draws out the whole range of stereotypical understandings about the person in the assignment. Generally students portray soldiers as men in uniform, terrorists as Muslim men of color, civilian victims of war as women and children, and trafficking victims as women tricked into sex work. The next step, of course is to criticize those stereotypes.

Group story-making activities almost always involve Popoki and *kamishibai*, a Japanese picture-story technique where the story-teller stands or sits behind large illustrations, traditionally in a special frame. Popoki's *kamishibai* sometimes include oral/written stories but are usually five-page silent stories. Like other group drawings, these stories must include Popoki. Some might be about specific topics; human rights stories, for example, would ask students to choose a particular right to illustrate and make a story about it. Often, students are shown a picture of Popoki crying or upset. They are asked to make stories about what upset Popoki, what the underlying causes are, and what they will do to help. A particular situation, topic or location can also be used: war, the right to peace, school, and so on. At the end, the stories are shared and discussed.

Popoki's activities are rooted in activism, but can be useful in the classroom to develop critical understandings of peace and war. The activities introduced above do not comprise a peace education curriculum. They are rather a selection of activities that can be used in a classroom or other setting to engage students and help them to think about various aspects of peace. I use these and other activities frequently in undergraduate and graduate school teaching and in workshops or seminars with people of all ages. Drawing and story-making are powerful tools for getting students to look inward and reflect, but also to look ahead and engage with imagining their desired future and how they might be able to help to create it.

All of the activities and ideas in these pages could be introduced and used without even mentioning Popoki's name or thinking about a cat, but the results might be very different. The magic of Popoki is that he is not human and therefore is not subject to the rules of human social relations. The real-life Popoki was male, but the Popoki Peace Project cat does not have a particular age, gender, social class, or identity; he is whatever the artist wants him to be. Sometimes he remains a cat, other times he becomes human or some other animal. He is also playful, and that playfulness can be used as an invitation to explore being different.

What is Popoki's role in teaching and creating peace? Popoki offers an inclusive and safe environment for exploring the concept of peace. Some students like Popoki because he is cute and different and it is only later that they realize they were engaged, sometimes in spite of themselves. Others appreciate the use of art and stories. Art-making and storytelling deepen our intellectual understanding of peace and war by adding a physical and sensorial dimension. It is a different perspective that might serve as an invitation to those students who are less interested or resistant, helping them to find something about peace that they consider meaningful. Many students comment that although they are interested in peace, it was not until engaging with Popoki that they thought about what it actually means. In fact, more than one student has confessed to me that with Popoki, for the first time peace seemed real, important, and perhaps most significantly, possible.

Learning and teaching peace often includes learning about war. In Japan, this often entails listening to first-hand accounts, something that can be painful for the teller and frightening for the listener. I have taught many university students who shy away from learning about peace because they were so overwhelmed by the survivor stories they heard in school. Popoki's approach is to draw out sensory images by, for example, asking a war or disaster survivor the color/taste/smell of her/his experience. This usually produces stories that are much more animated and accessible than most survivor testimonies, although they can also be very horrifying as in a story of an eight-year-old who described the smell of war as the smell of blood. Because these sensory images are so compelling, Popoki is careful to follow up and to comfort those for whom remembering, and listening, is painful.

(Multiple Popokis from a peace camp in Timor Leste, Summer, 2007)
(2016.12 Story from Rights of the Child Workshop).

Popoki works on an everyday basis with young people who are struggling to find their place in a violent and confusing world. He played a central role at a week-long international peace camp held in Timor Leste during a period of violence and helped to keep young Timorese men talking about peace rather than going out to fight. The young men ultimately arranged a football game with their political rivals. A workshop for staff at a mental health clinic in Palestine began on a negative note when the director informed me that Palestinians do not like cats, but wound up with her asking that I leave some drawings because Popoki could be a symbol of hope. On Okinawa and Guam, islands grappling with militarization and colonization, Popoki's questions help people to think about their land and culture and to question whether the military presence on their islands really makes them safer. And in communities suffering from disaster and radioactive contamination in northeastern Japan, the Marshall Islands, Hiroshima, and Nagasaki, Popoki listens carefully to each story, learning, sharing, and trying to help ensure that they are not forgotten. He stands in solidarity with all of those communities, but he understands that change, if and when it comes, must come from within.

Popoki is not always successful. Some students find him to be too cute, or too playful, or think that Popoki himself and/or the act of drawing are too childish. Some students feel threatened by the open-ended approach, particularly when they cannot predict the expected answer. In some cases, group work makes it easier because the collective decision making means there is less chance of being wrong. In contrast, among those who enjoy the creative challenge are students who prefer to work alone because having to negotiate a collective storyline interferes with their own expression. There are always students who resist, and some who refuse to become a part of the group. Most of the time, however, those students are watching, even as they claim disinterest.

Teaching peace means challenging ourselves to imagine and to create a different future, even when it seems there is not any reason for hope. Popoki has become an indispensable part of my teaching, learning, and activism, partly because he reminds me to look for hidden rainbows. Each class and workshop is different, but Popoki is always there to help us imagine what peace might look like, and to remind us to believe in the possibility of a better tomorrow.

RECOMMENDED READINGS

Alexander, Ronni. 2012. "Remembering Hiroshima: Bio-Politics, Popoki and Sensual Expressions of War." *International Feminist Journal of Politics* 14 (2): 202–222. doi:10.1080/14616742.2012.659852.

Wada, Kenji. 2011. "Conversations with Ronni Alexander: The Popoki Peace Project: Popoki, What Color is Peace? What Color is Friendship?" *International Feminist Journal of Politics* 13 (2): 257–271.

Teaching Peace Education at a South African University

VAUGHN M. JOHN

Any reflections on teaching peace and war will invariably be shaped by the context in which such teaching occurs, by the teacher, and by a vision of the world that such teaching seeks to promote. Thus, I begin with the ingredients that shape my teaching of peace education courses at the University of KwaZulu-Natal in South Africa.

During the 1980s, I joined my university, located in a province gripped by a deadly civil conflict. This conflict, ostensibly between rival political organizations, claimed approximately 7,500 lives and was later known as the Natal War. For the first six years, I worked on a project that monitored and reported on the conflict during emergency law restrictions, which sought to conceal the Apartheid state's funding and incitement of this violence. We also provided support to displaced persons. This worked sensitized me to the processes of enemy-making and war-mongering, and the importance of peace education as a counter force and restorative process. When the violence ended, we developed conflict resolution workshops for affected communities, and later, formal university courses in Peace Education and Conflict Resolution. The following discusses the formal courses at undergraduate and master's levels that I have developed and revised over the last fifteen years, and my approach to teaching peace education in this post-conflict context.

The context in which I teach is one that is still deeply divided, with ongoing politically motivated murders. This violence occurs in a nation that is racially divided despite the formal abolition of Apartheid. Criminal and gender-based violence are also at exceptionally high levels. The Statistician General recently released figures from a Victims of Crime Survey (2016/17) that indicated 15,256 murders, 58,013 sexual offenses, and 53,003 vehicle hijackings in South Africa, which has a population of some 55 million people. He reported alarming (and contested) rates of increase of 9 percent, 117 percent, and 93 percent, respectively, for these three categories of crime. Much of this physical violence stems from deep-seated structural violence, including high levels of unemployment and poverty. These conditions are associated with long histories of exploitation and oppression in South Africa. Schools reflect the levels of division and violence in broader society. The students attending my courses are educators in these schools and communities and often feel concerned yet helpless regarding their capacity to intervene. They have developed certain mindsets about their context, about themselves, and their roles as teachers that limit capacity to be peace educators.

Part of these mindsets relate to how Africa and South Africa are seen, and to limited understandings of conflict and peace. The very notion of peace education is often encountered for the first time in these courses. The levels of violence in society create cultures of fear, hopelessness, and polarization. This dominance of violence has demanded a curriculum with a focus on nonviolence and practical conflict resolution skills. The mindsets of educators have required a pedagogy that fosters critical thinking, while building hope, caring, and most importantly, agency. But how does one do this within the institutional constraints of limited face-to-face engagement with part-time students who attend class once per week over a short semester? How does one blend theory and practice and combine reflection with action? And how does one attempt to assess all of this in a manner that promotes learning and action, while still meeting institutional requirements?

Curriculum content, pedagogy, and assignments developed in response to the contextual and institutional influences just identified will be presented here. I will discuss: the need to build practical conflict resolution skills and a connection to a community of peace practice; the need to change the narrative about "violent Africa and South Africa" and the inevitability of violence; and how I have dealt with limited class time by flipping the classroom using an innovative Conflict Mapping project that serves as a capstone assignment. I will first set out the philosophy guiding teaching of peace education.

M y approach to teaching is guided by critical theory, transformative learning theory, and the inclusion of African perspectives and practices of peacebuilding. In this I draw on the work of Paulo Freire, Jack Mezirow, Gabo Nsteane, bell hooks, Frantz Fanon, Achille Mbembe, and Mamood Mamdani. I also present African leaders like Nelson Mandela, Steve Biko, and Desmond Tutu as sources of wisdom and indigenous knowledge on practical peacemaking and justice.

First, I believe a key role is to engage students in reflecting critically on their perspectives and habitual mindsets that shape their understandings and actions in life. In South Africa, given our violent history of colonialism and apartheid, as well as entrenched systems of patriarchy and neoliberalism, such socialization is marked significantly by oppression, exploitation, and trauma. These mindsets are the products of years of oppressive socialization. Such a context requires that education must foster critical reflection on one's mindsets with a view to transforming perspectives that are false or limiting, and which do not sustain people and the planet. This important agenda has been brought to the fore by movements to "decolonize" the mind and curriculum. Below, I will show examples of how I employ critical pedagogy and participatory methodology to trigger critical reflection on mindsets, build Afrocentric perspectives, and to thereafter enable students to implement action based on their revised perspectives within an African post-conflict context with high levels of violence.

A second feature of my approach is thus to combine reflection with action. This is fundamental to equipping educators to build what Freire referred to as a critical praxis, the productive harmonizing of theory and practice and the creation of agency. The conflict mapping projects I discuss below best illustrate this aspect of my approach. Linking students to communities of peace practice, also expanded below, is another important way of inviting and supporting students in developing their own praxis.

A third aspect of my teaching approach is to foster creative, caring and democratic educational spaces. Here I am guided by African feminist theorists on caring and humanizing pedagogy and by Freire's teaching on building hopeful pedagogy. My own scholarship on theorizing adult education in post-conflicts as care work has extended this exploration. I believe that structural violence has eroded values of care, interdependence, and a common humanity. Much of the exceedingly negative and disabling narratives about Africa fail to acknowledge the longer historical roots of contemporary conflict as well as the indigenous systems that nurture life and humanity. Peace education can play a role in challenging and building new narratives.

I will illustrate the above approach primarily with reference to a master's level course on Peace Education and Conflict Resolution, as well as related undergraduate courses. The next section reveals plans to provide practical conflict resolution skills and connection to a community of practice through the Alternative to Violence Project (AVP).

E ducators need to learn practical conflict resolution skills that they can practice in their lives and develop in their learners. There are many courses and learning materials that support the development of these skills. In earlier versions of my courses I have included lessons and role-plays on negotiation, mediation, and other conflict resolution skills. Over the last decade I have managed to integrate some non-formal courses, the AVP, into my university courses. AVP offers a set of powerful and practical courses on nonviolent conflict resolution. There are three levels of courses, namely, AVP Basic, AVP Advanced, and Training for Facilitators. These courses have been run in communities, schools, and prisons in approximately sixty countries around the world. The inclusion of AVP in teaching for peace has brought several benefits.

AVP comes with an established curriculum and manuals that guide facilitators on how to teach nonviolent conflict resolution using highly participatory pedagogy. While there are core principles and learning objectives, there are a variety of exercises that can be selected to suit particular groups and learning environments. Importantly, AVP encourages customization and local-adaptations leading to incorporation of indigenous knowledge and practices.

A second significant advantage of including AVP is that educators are not only provided with an established curriculum and pedagogy for teaching practical peacemaking, they are also connected to a community of peace educators. The benefits of stand-alone peacemaking courses can easily be lost in an environment that does not provide ongoing support and development of novice peace educators. AVP deals with this challenge by inviting participants in the Basic course to complete the Advanced course and then gain training in how to facilitate an AVP workshop in the third level course.

Once trained as a facilitator, one can get involved in facilitating AVP workshops under the guidance of more experienced facilitators. Novices thus learn and grow within a supportive and committed community of peace educators. In my university courses, I have often included former students to run the AVP component as a way of connecting current and former students, and illustrating the kinds of skills and identity development that are involved in the journey of becoming a peace educator. Research with AVP facilitators has shown that facilitators value AVP's established practical curriculum and supportive community of practice.

Bringing community-based, non-formal courses into university programs challenges conventional understandings of knowledge exchange and expertise, and can create symbiotic and durable linkages between university-based, school-based, and community-based educators. As my teaching of peace education is tied to my community engagement and research, I have been able to create synergies across these work domains. This allows for students to receive practical training in nonviolent conflict resolution and enables peace praxis. Some of these educators are now involved in peace work and four past students are employed as school-based peace club facilitators in a project that I support. To further this scholarship, I have developed three research projects on local peace practices within which some of my postgraduate students have conducted their research. I will now illustrate my attempts to change the narrative about "violent Africa and South Africa."

Violence is dehumanizing for perpetrators, victims, and society at large. Endemic violence as experienced in South Africa erodes hope, agency, and belief in humanity. It becomes easy to believe that violence is inevitable and that nothing can be done to prevent it. Processes of fear, apathy, and blaming reduce one's personal sense of responsibility and agency. Yet in truth most

South Africans and their neighbors on the continent live peacefully. This often occurs despite living with deep injustices and structural violence. There are also many wonderful daily examples of peacemaking and peacebuilding by ordinary people that are not covered by the media in the ways that violence is reported on, or in the ways that peace icons are profiled.

In response to this I have infused African perspectives, practices, and case studies in my peace education courses by drawing on African authors, including guest lecturers and student's presentations, and by linking this to my own scholarship on African peacebuilding projects and peacemakers. I see this as an important counterbalance to the deluge of violence and war journalism we receive, and an exceedingly Eurocentric-dominated literature and practice in the field of peace. I offer two examples of this building of African perspectives and practices in peace education.

In 2014, on the first anniversary of the death of Nelson Mandela, I recognized the need to assert his prominence, not just as a world-renown peacemaker, but also as a great thinker and theorist on peace and reconciliation. Mandela's celebratory status is not matched by the development of literature, scholarship, and course offerings that portray him as a theorist and source of great wisdom. Other peace icons like Mahatma Gandhi and Martin Luther King have given rise to a vast scholarship and a range of course offerings globally. There is a need to develop a critical scholarship and teaching based on the life and work of Nelson Mandela and other liberatory thinkers like Steve Biko. Recognizing this gap, I developed a paper on Mandela's peace wisdom for the International Peace Research Association conference. I also contributed an article to the Global Campaign for Peace Education newsletter on lessons from Mandela. Both of these are now resources within my peace education courses.

A second example is the inclusion of local non-formal peacebuilding practices, like AVP, into my formal courses. Likewise, past courses have exposed students to a local community-based mediation project called Zwelethemba. Practitioners of these community-based peacemaking interventions are invited to class to speak to students or run workshops for them.

Video and Internet-based technology provides another means to showcase peacebuilding perspectives and practices from Africa, and to link local and global struggles. I regularly use videos to support my teaching. For example, *The Wajir Story* illustrates how a group of women in Northern Kenya initiated peacebuilding and peace education in an endemic conflict. It conveys a counterhegemonic message that disrupts mindsets about conflict in Africa and the role of women in strong patriarchal and religious societies. It also displays African wisdom and practices, conveying a hopeful message of possibility and agency for peace educators. Student evaluations reveal appreciation for the use of video within a variety of teaching methods employed, as reflected in the following comments from students, "I enjoyed the different styles of teaching methods used such as videos, documentaries, AVP, class cooperation, etc. Seminars were extremely useful," and "I really enjoyed the variety of resources and teaching methods used e.g. slides, videos, discussions, drawing, reflective practices." Peace pedagogy requires such variety and participatory methods.

A further example of using video with Internet technology was a class I ran with a colleague in Japan where we connected our students via Skype for a joint class. The students exchanged experiences of conflict and war experienced by their families in both countries. The value of this exercise was to get students to share common experiences and thereby link local and global experiences of war and violence. The students enjoyed this exchange and through this created a video resource for future classes. The next section will discuss pedagogy that allows for "flipping the classroom" using a Conflict Mapping project.

As indicated, my teaching is with part-time adult students who attend for day-long sessions. A typical six-hour session thus requires careful advanced preparations. This includes readings and activities prior to the class sessions and combinations of lectures, group work, participatory activities, videos and student presentations in class. As mentioned earlier, participatory activities include the use of role-play, scenarios, games, and student-led engagement. Given the scheduling constraints for part-time students, I have successfully introduced a multistage conflict-mapping project that allows for the classroom to be flipped, and for opportunities for critical reflection, participatory learning, and the development of a peace praxis.

In both undergraduate and master's courses, I have developed an innovative multistage conflict mapping project that flips the classroom such that students do lower level cognitive tasks (reading and collecting data from their contexts) outside of class, and engage in higher forms of cognitive work (analyzing, evaluating, and creating) in a collaborative class environment. This flipped classroom creates a dynamic space for applying knowledge to their real-world context, discussing, comparing, and critically analyzing mindsets and contexts. This leads to the design of peace education lessons and actions to address conflict and injustice in their school and community contexts.

Elsewhere I have reported more fully on how I use conflict mapping to foster critical thinking and the development of a peace praxis with my students. A summary of the steps of the mapping project in a flipped classroom is provided below.

Step 1: Gets students to map their school and to analyze this context in terms of conflict, violence, and injustice. This allows for learning and assessment of authentic and situated learning on real-life contexts.

Step 2: Students get their pupils to do a similar task and they engage with their pupils on how they experience the school. They are asked to get male and female pupils to do this mapping separately. This allows for the learning and assessment of what Freire promotes as dialogic learning and horizontal, respectful engagement between teacher and learner. This gives practical meaning to being both teacher-learners and learner-teachers. This also provides opportunity to explore the school as a gendered space.

Step 3: This important step requires students to compare their own maps with that of their pupils' maps. This becomes a powerful opportunity to teach and assess critical reflection on mindsets and blind spots. Here students are guided and challenged to give attention to their assumptions and frameworks, which filter what they see and do not see, and to acknowledge the effects of socialization, oppression, structural violence, and systems like patriarchy and power. This step allows for gender, class, and age differences to be explored.

Step 4: This step gets students to plan peace education and peace action interventions for a key problem identified in the pupils' maps. It provides space for the learning and assessment objectives related to developing a peace praxis (combining reflection and action), selection and application of course content on peace curricula, and development of a peace educator identity. In the most recent offering of this course, this step was turned into a group project. Students worked in groups of three and four to develop the peace education and action interventions. While this was in part prompted by an unusually large class in 2017, it also provided space for group work and learning, which is important in peace education. Two groups not only developed interventions, but also piloted them at their institutions.

Step 5: At a "conflict mapping conference" students present these projects in class before the final submission of the capstone project. They are granted an opportunity to engage in dialogue with other students and share their learning. This allows for another level of comparison and building of a composite view of the contexts of teaching and learning in South Africa. Students are also given opportunities to develop presentation and media skills. They benefit from formative feedback from myself and fellow students. Formative feedback is also provided at two prior stages when students present their maps and pupils' maps in class and during class discussions on map comparisons. These presentations are assessed according to criteria negotiated in class. In this way I allow students to be involved in contributing to the criteria for part of their assessment, a demonstration of democratic teaching and learning strategies promoted in peace education.

Step 6: The mapping project guidelines stipulate that students are required to engage in literature beyond that provided in the course and to comply with institutional writing and referencing requirements. Students are given time to revise and submit their final project based on feedback received. Some students are given a second opportunity for revision before projects are sent to the external examiner. The external examiner has found the mapping projects to be a novel way to teach and assess peace education.

The project promotes higher levels of cognitive processes. While students initially engage in description of their contexts they quickly move into analysis and comparison of contexts and causes. They are required to apply conflict analysis skills and peace education skills in the project. Together the project moves them into synthesis, evaluation, and creation as they bring all the elements of the project together in generating data on their real day-to-day context, identifying and analyzing problems and developing solutions.

Several students have gone on to implement their peace education plans and have picked up on some of the mapping findings for their dissertation research. An example of this is Busi Mabaso, who wrote about how her mapping project generated her interest in wanting to explore sexual violence for her master's thesis. The mapping project had served to conscientize her about her school context and her role within an oppressive context. She wrote:

> The level of uneasiness, reluctance to report and discouraging comments from both learners and teachers to pursue this issue created my desire to know more about this sensitive issue [sexual violence]. Keeping quiet and being guilty of colluding with the oppressors at the expense of vulnerable learners meant I had become 'host' to my own oppression an idea which Paulo Freire (1995) warns of. These unacceptable practices had potential to divide the school, affect learners and teachers emotionally and academically and thus affect the smooth running of the school.

The mapping projects and other activities discussed generate situated learning, collaborative explorations, and critical reflections on the lived realities of students' schools and communities. It advances many of my objectives in teaching peace education, including: fostering critical thinking and multiple forms of dialogue; embracing diversity of views and recognizing one's blindspots; inviting students into the identity of peace educator and to peace communities; positioning educators as agents of change and care; praxis-oriented: involving multiple stages of reflection and action; intervention-oriented: integrating peace theory and practice for change, focusing on authentic African contexts and challenges. There are also some indications that these courses challenge students, develop new mindsets, and create interest in the possibilities of peace education in a post-conflict and violent context.

RECOMMENDED READING

John, Vaughn M. 2016 "Using Conflict Mapping to Foster Peace-Related Learning and Change in Schools." *Education as Change* 20 (2): 221–242. doi:10.17159/1947-9417/2016/756.

Participatory Action Research For Peacebuilding

SYLVIA KAYE AND GEOFF HARRIS

For many years, as supervisors of postgraduate research projects, we encouraged exploratory research—uncovering and developing new knowledge—in the hope that this would somehow bring about social change. The way in which research is conducted and reported, however, limits the awareness of such knowledge to a very small group of people, usually the student, the supervisor, and the examiners. Those with power to bring about change are unlikely to become aware of research findings or, if they do, only after long delays. In consequence, the people about whom the research was conducted are not likely to benefit.

In recent years, the need we felt for research findings to be translated into action became increasingly insistent. This has led us to encourage our students to undertake action research (AR)/participatory action research (PAR) as a means of actually bringing about change. The most obvious benefit of action research is that some peace is built immediately, albeit usually for small numbers of people, as students go through the process of exploring a problem, devising and implementing an intervention, and evaluating its outcome. It is also possible that the micro-level outcomes typically sought in action research might spread more widely. There is in fact no reason why action research cannot be employed to bring about macro-level change, given that its sequence of exploring, planning, acting, and reflecting can apply to any level of social endeavor.

Action research provides a key tool for peacebuilding because it includes the community as participants and direct beneficiaries. We discuss the meanings and rationale for action research, present some AR case studies from our students, and consider some of the challenges it faces.

While there is no single definition of AR, it is clear that it involves research, so as to arrive at new knowledge and understandings, reflection and action to bring about change. Another central feature is collaboration with, and the participation of, the people who are experiencing the problem.

The balance between action and reflection resolves two problems common to research—an overemphasis on data collection or an emphasis on action without an adequate research foundation.

Action research has existed for generations in an informal sense, as so often communities solved problems through a similar process. Communities typically relied on collaborative and participatory activities, and would identify a problem, plan and carry out a solution, and reflect on the efficacy of the solution. Kurt Lewin is credited with developing a more formal meaning of action research during the 1940s. He concluded that there was often great good-will within communities, but also uncertainty of what could be done to bring about change. He was aware that research alone would not produce much by way of change. In Lewin's words, "Mere diagnosis—and surveys are a type of diagnosis—does not suffice." That is, action has to be taken and researchers are in a good position to encourage such action.

The process of action research has been described as being recursive and nonlinear, with the answer unknown. Commonly, however, there are four phases, once the problem has been identified. First, exploring the problem by collecting and analyzing relevant data (this is where most research ends); second, planning an intervention to tackle the problem; third, implementing the intervention; fourth, evaluating the outcomes. Reflection on both the process of the intervention and the outcomes may result in a new understanding of the problem and may result in a further iteration of action research.

In our supervision of doctoral students in peacebuilding from across Africa, we insist on the use of action research. We have found that the topics they then choose fall into a number of categories—education/training, healing, reconciliation, restorative justice, and building peace infrastructures. Summaries of four such projects will clarify and extend this overview of the action research process and illustrate its role in peacebuilding.

Jean de Dieu Basabose's project concerned anti-corruption education as a way of building positive peace in Rwanda. In explaining the research problem, he wrote that corruption has increasingly undermined peacebuilding processes. Anti-corruption efforts therefore constitute one of the ways of building and sustaining positive peace. Attempts to combat corruption generally follow one of three approaches—developing legal and punitive frameworks to act as a deterrent, devising bureaucratic structures that make its practice more difficult, and promoting ethical values-based approaches. This action research project was designed to test whether anti-corruption concepts and practices could be taught to primary school children, and to gain insights into their possible future behavior concerning corruption.

The project began by exploring the nature, causes, and extent of the problem, using a series of interviews with relevant stakeholders and focus group discussions. The intervention stage was to develop and test an educational curriculum for primary school children focusing on anti-corruption. Four modules were developed covering the concept of corruption; healthy and clean wealth; civic responsibility; and values needed in making ethical choices. Teacher-facilitators were trained to teach 12 lessons to 60 children over a six-month period. Some of the challenges faced during the research were fatalistic beliefs on the part of parents that corruption was next to impossible to root out, and time requirements. In terms of outcomes, learners regarded the training very positively, while parents thought that the training needed to be longer and ongoing. The overall finding of the study was that such training is likely to contribute to more ethical behavior as regards corruption when the learners became adults.

In summarizing his project, Basabose explained that action research creates an opportunity for people—including the researcher—to think about a real community problem, explore resources existing in their communities, and play an important role in collaboratively responding to it. It inspires participants to take responsibility and own the process of addressing a problem, it creatively engages them in finding appropriate solutions and establishing preventive or promotional mechanisms to help secure the future they want.

Buhlebenkosi Maphosa's project was concerned to develop ways to reduce gender-based violence among Zimbabwean youth. In describing the research problem, Maphosa explained that gender-based violence (GBV) includes all forms of violence that disproportionately targets women and girls, including dating violence, domestic violence, sexual assault, and intimate partner violence. GBV is Zimbabwe's most important social concern for women and the major form of violence in the country.

The study began by investigating learner's attitudes toward GBV in two secondary schools—one rural, one urban—in the Bulawayo area, using a survey questionnaire and focus group discussions. An action research group of 12 participants was created at each of the schools to help design, implement, and evaluate a GBV prevention program. Their intervention was a series of workshops using drama, songs, and poetry, and was presented to around 40 students in each school. Responses by learners showed their appreciation of the workshop content; they urged that such interventions would become part of the school curriculum because it provided a space for them to discuss the GBV challenges they faced.

Even so, Buhle noted that it was difficult to develop initiative among the action group as they explored and shared ideas on interventions that would address GBV. She believed this came from a strong expectation to be taught and directed, as they were used to in the formal school setting, and she had to work hard to encourage them to value their own suggestions and see their role as important.

An "elephant in the room" in Zimbabwe is the tension between the Shona and Ndebele ethnic groups. There is, of course, a history underlying this tension, dating from the arrival of the Ndebele in what is now Zimbabwe. More recent events include the *Gukurahundi* massacres of the 1980s and the belief by the Ndbele that they receive much less from the government than do the Shona. Considerable tension and limited cooperation are the hallmarks of present day Shona–Ndebele relations and these are passed on from generation to generation.

Cyprian Muchemwa's action research project was aimed at building understanding and reconciliation between Shona and Ndebele young people. To this end, he brought together a mixed group of twelve university students aged 18 to 25 who engaged in six dialogue sessions over a five-month period. These formed an experimental group, and changes in them were tested using before versus after comparisons with a control group of similar students. He found that listening to the "other" in an attempt to understand them, rather than to win the argument, was an effective way of breaking down suspicion and tension. Cyprian regards this as a "slight shift from pessimism to cautious optimism." Participants felt that they had become victims of a polarization that was not of their own making.

In the Great Lakes region of Africa since the mid-1990s, tens of thousands of child soldiers have been recruited, some by force, but most voluntarily, into government and militia forces. When they leave these forces and want to return to their families and communities, important questions of accountability and justice emerge. Should they just be accepted back, should they be rejected altogether, or should they face some form of justice in order to pay a price for their actions? Chrys Kiyala examined the potential role of the *baraza*, the traditional community conflict resolution and restorative justice mechanism used, in varying forms, throughout central and east Africa. In areas subject to armed conflict and displacement of populations, however, it has lost much of its vigor. In practice, *baraza* involves community meetings where any member is able to speak, and where an offender is able to admit his or her behavior and to ask for forgiveness. Could it be strengthened to enable its use in a new role, that of helping the child soldier offenders and their victims achieve an acceptable level of justice?

Working with four war-affected communities in the North Kivu Province of eastern Democratic Republic of the Congo, Chrys introduced peacemaking circles into the *baraza* process. He found that that three quarters of 282 community members who were involved with these circles accepted that this restorative approach was sufficient to allow the reintegration of former child soldiers. Chrys followed this up with training for other communities (1,165 people in total) in the principles and practice of peacemaking circles and restorative justice.

As well as illustrating the range of peacebuilding issues to which action research can be applied, these case studies point to some general challenges that action researchers face. First, given the traditional emphasis on exploratory research with its positivist underpinnings, a research proposal based on action research may well be criticized as not being research, but rather, "what consultants do." Related to this is a concern that a detailed plan cannot normally be provided for action research projects because the precise direction the research will go is not known at the start; this is particularly the case when the project's participants are strongly involved in planning and implementation.

Second, when the research forms part or the whole of the requirements for a degree, there is a requirement to complete it within some minimum time. Given the necessity of careful exploration before an intervention is planned, let alone implemented, it is often not possible to complete an action research project quickly. This is one reason why students typically opt to only explore a problem, in which case the research is best regarded as an academic exercise that is unlikely to result in any change for the better (it might be possible to shortcut the whole process, provided good quality, explorative research has been previously carried out, by beginning to design an intervention almost immediately). This also explains why most action research projects stop at the end of one iteration and do not go on to repeat the intervention in modified form(s).

Third, action researchers are committed to follow principles of participation, collaboration, and democracy in their research, and so face much more than the usual problems that confront field researchers. It is one thing to collect data from people in order to explore a problem, but quite another to involve them in using these data to plan, implement, and evaluate an intervention. Facilitating a genuine role for participants in shaping a project will inevitably be time-consuming, and may take the project down unexpected and possibly undesired pathways, but action research asks researchers to be catalysts and facilitators rather than controllers. Unless researchers make participation central, the wisdom and energy of the participants will lie largely untapped. This said, the potential of an outsider as a catalyst should not be under-valued. There are often instances where individuals and communities are stuck in situations and are not able or willing to make the first moves to tackle it. An outsider can provide the initial impetus for movement forward and can help keep the ensuing process moving.

A fourth challenge is how to do action research and collect data at the same time. An action research thesis requires an account of the planning, implementing, and evaluation processes and, more importantly, the student's analytical reflections on these. It will also very likely require data collected from conventional methods—surveys, in-depth interviews, focus groups, and above all, observation—that need to be carefully carried out. Any performance indicators to be used to evaluate whether change has occurred need to be devised, and initial data collected, before any interventions begin. This dual task of ensuring that good data is being collected while maintaining the principles of participation and collaboration is demanding.

These challenges emphasize the value of an advisory/support group for the researcher, particularly for the more participatory projects.

Two final points can be made. One concerns the critical distinction between conflict management, conflict resolution, and conflict transformation. Managing a conflict often involves separating the protagonists, whereas efforts at resolution try to find a deal which is acceptable to the parties in conflict. As Jean Paul Lederach continually reminds us, however, resolution may change very little in the sense that the parties may continue to hold the same attitudes of fear, anger, and mistrust toward each other. Projects that involve parties from different sides of a conflict in action research have some potential to transform such attitudes over time.

The second is the need to remain aware of the often toxic influence of the social and economic systems under which participants live. Action research can help develop a culture where conflicts are resolved and, hopefully, relationships transformed, but there is a level that it only rarely touches—the structurally violent systems in which human interactions are played out. Sarah Henkeman has discussed this in the context of workplace conflicts between employers, who hold most of the power, and the employees, who have much less. How can conflicts be resolved let alone transformed under conditions of gross economic inequality, disempowerment, and oppression? How can the reach of action research be extended to include these systems?

RECOMMENDED READINGS

Basabose, Jean de Dieu. 2017. "Anti-Corruption Education as a Way of Building Positive Peace in Rwanda." In Sylvia Kaye and Geoff Harris (eds.), *Building Peace via Action Research: African Case Studies*. Addis Ababa, Ethiopia: University for Peace. Available at: <http://www.icon.org.za/current/wp-content/uploads/2017/12/Building-Peace-via-Action-Research2c-2017.pdf>, last accessed December 6, 2017.

Henkeman, Sarah. 2010. "Mediator's Dilemma: Mediation in South Africa—An Unequal, Deeply Divided, Transitional Society." *Tesseract for norsk psykologforening* (Special Edition on Mediation) 47:731–733.

Johnson, Andrew. 2011. *A Short Guide to Action Research*. 4th edition. Boston, MA: Allyn and Bacon.

Kiyala, Jean Chrysostome Kiyala. 2017. "Reintegrating Former Child Soldiers: An Action Research Project in the Eastern Democratic Republic of Congo." In Sylvia Kaye and Geoff Harris (eds.), *Building Peace via Action Research: African Case Studies*, 223–238. Addis Ababa, Ethiopia. Available at <http://www.icon.org.za/current/wp-content/uploads/2017/12/Building-Peace-via-Action-Research2c-2017.pdf>, last accessed December 6, 2017.

Lederach, Jean Paul. 2003. *The Little Book of Conflict Transformation*. Intercourse, PA: Good Books.

Lewin, Kurt. 1946. "Action Research and Minority Problems." *Journal of Social Issues* 2 (4): 34–46. doi:10.1111/j.1540-4560.1946.tb02295.x

McNiff, Jean, and Jack Whitehead. 2011. *All You Need to Know about Action Research*. 2nd edition. London: Sage Publications.

Maphosa, Buhlebenkosi. 2017. "Reducing Gender-Based Violence: Action Research among Zimbabwean Youth." In Sylvia Kaye and Geoff Harris (eds.), *Building Peace via Action Research: African Case Studies*, 95–118. Addis Ababa, Ethiopia: University for Peace. Available at <http://www.icon.org.za/current/wp-content/uploads/2017/12/Building-Peace-via-Action-Research2c-2017.pdf>, last accessed December 6, 2017.

Muchemwa, Cyprian. 2017. "Moving Towards Reconciliation using Action Research: Ndebele and Shona Relations in Zimbabwe." In Sylvia Kaye and Geoff Harris (eds.), *Building Peace via Action Research: African Case Studies*, 143–166. Addis Ababa, Ethiopia: University for Peace. Available at <http://www.icon.org.za/current/wp-content/uploads/2017/12/Building-Peace-via-Action-Research2c-2017.pdf>, last accessed December 6, 2017.

Reason, Peter, and Hilary Bradbury (eds.). 2008. *Handbook of Action Research: Participative Inquiry and Practice*. 2nd edition. London: Sage Publications.

Teaching Counterfactuals from Hell

ANJALI KAUSHLESH DAYAL AND PAUL MUSGRAVE

Undergraduate students' interest in war, conflict, and peace often springs from their quest to understand a particular conflict, or to know how a policy might lessen bloodshed and human suffering. These desires sustain them through the arduous task of mastering the details of what actually took place in a given conflict or mass atrocity. Understandably, once details about some representative cases have been communicated, students then often want to leap from the particulars of those cases into more general theorizing about why wars take place or what the effect of given policy interventions aimed at reducing harms would be.

The students' natural desire to want to change the world based on what they have learned about it poses a pedagogical challenge when that motive meets professors' desire to acknowledge the limits of what we know. Students, we have found, can be dissatisfied with their professors' reluctance to convey certainty, and uncomfortable with the techniques scholars use to contend with this uncertainty. Driven to understand and to help, students often become frustrated with their instructors' refusal to say how a particular genocide could have been (or could be) prevented, and discomfited by nuanced conclusions that a particular form of intervention might be helpful in some circumstances but unhelpful in others.

S tudents inspired by the idea of studying war and peace often begin their investigations from the same point of view as many pundits and policy makers: that there exist timeless and invariant "lessons of history" that, like mathematical proofs, can be indefinitely applied once derived. Instructors who seek to engage with students must begin by addressing this unexamined assumption. Guiding students to the recognition that some questions are unanswerable requires helping them to understand the fundamental problem of casual inference: that we cannot know for certain what the effect of a given intervention was, or would have been, since we cannot observe both the world in which that intervention took place and a world entirely alike except for the intervention.

As social scientists engaged in a theoretical enterprise, we spend our time thinking as much—or more—about what we can learn from events that never happened as we do about the "lessons of history" commonly described. Thinking and teaching about peace and war requires thinking not just about the conflicts that took place and the policies that were chosen in response, but also about the conflicts that never took place and policy choices that could have been made but were not. For many social scientists, the point of methodological training is devising ways to grapple with the possibilities of counterfactual history—what might have been but never was—to estimate the causal effect of choices and factors. These "lessons of unhistory" underpin all of our analyses but require analytical styles unfamiliar to most undergraduates (or, for that matter, most people).

Consider some reasonable questions that students (or policy makers) might ask: How effective was North Atlantic Treaty Organization (NATO) intervention in Libya? How effective has UN involvement in the Democratic Republic of the Congo (DRC), Haiti, and Sudan been? Would the DRC, Haiti, and Sudan have been better off without UN involvement? How many lives could the United States have saved if it had intervened in Syria's civil war earlier? Can the international community stop ongoing genocides? From students' perspectives, it appears reasonable to expect that experts who know all the details about what did happen should be able to answer these questions.

Teaching students to evaluate these questions requires serious thought about how to teach troubling counterfactuals. If students operate from a "deficit model" that holds that the difference between an expert and a nonexpert is simply the volume of information that experts possess, then they will expect that an expert can supply the necessary data to fill in the gaps. And yet many experts (ourselves included) would respond that answering any of these questions is impossible without considering how bad a given situation would have been in the absence of intervention.

Teaching students to grapple with these cases requires preparing them for the unique ethical, methodological, and epistemological concerns that follow from counterfactual analysis of the realities of intervention in difficult contexts. For many students, driven by an impulse toward justice and protection of the innocent, academics' insistence that we question whether a posited intervention would have worked, or whether an actually existing intervention did save the lives its supporters claim, can appear not just frustrating but immoral. Yet we believe that only analyses grounded in such detached considerations can offer suitable policy prescriptions, no matter how engaged we may wish to be in employing those analyses to alleviate human suffering.

Designing syllabi, classes, and research assignments with these challenges in mind requires preparing students to address the vexing problems of weighing both policy options and structural variables on horrible situations that have no "good" outcomes. We address each of these challenges in turn.

First, there are ethical concerns. It can be difficult to say whether an intervention in a mass atrocity situation "worked" or not. Studying interventions intended to bring peace or protection involves a grotesque but necessary calculus of evaluating outcomes. Because we cannot understand the effects of intervention without weighing relative scales of devastation and recognizing the absence of a feasible utopian outcome, we have to ask monstrous questions like: Would death have come faster, more painfully, more extensively without an intervention? Or did more people die because of the intervention?

All strategies in situations of conflict and mass violence may be only the best of bad options. Thinking through counterfactual reasoning can help students reconcile the fact that even policy successes may be human tragedies—and that sometimes intervention may be counterproductive. Even if the international community intervenes, the continuation of killing does not mean that an intervention failed. Given that the baseline expectation once a process of mass violence begins is already cataclysmic, even a "successful" intervention will probably fail to save many people. By the same token, noting that atrocities continued in the absence of intervention is not itself evidence that intervention is effective.

Consider debates over the efficacy of UN peacekeeping. Aggregate statistical work tells us that UN peacekeeping is a highly effective tool when combatants have signed an agreement. Case studies, popular conceptions of peacekeeping, and the actual number of failed missions (roughly 1 in 4) paint a slightly more confusing picture. Should students (and policymakers) conclude that UN peacekeeping is an effective tool for ensuring a stable post-conflict peace? If 1 out of 4 airline flights crashed, we would end commercial aviation. But if peacekeeping is a last-ditch effort to resolve an intractable conflict, then in 3 out of 4 cases that receive peacekeeping operations, not sliding back into war could be a reasonable success rate—even if the peace itself is imperfect, and even if the single failure comes with untold death and suffering. The better analogy is to, say, cancer treatments, in which interventions should be evaluated relative to the set of mostly undesirable plausible outcomes. How should we understand a treatment that saves 3 out of 4 patients if it kills the fourth patient—or one that cures cancer in 3 out of 4 patients, only with potentially life-altering side effects? Here, empirical analysis slides into ethical judgments, but at least we can proceed on a firmer analogy.

In our experience, students often find it difficult to discuss these calculations. They often find the logic of triage to be ethically fraught at best or abhorrent at worst. For many students, the imperative of doing something, anything, to end suffering is a common refrain. The widespread use in college classrooms of Samantha Power's excellent *A Problem from Hell*, with its focus on political will as the key stumbling block to meaningful atrocity prevention and its emphasis on a "toolbox" of possible policy options for genocide response, reinforces this idea.

It is not just students who have such reactions. In August 2017, for example, the U.S. Holocaust Museum's Simon-Skjodt Center for the Prevention of Genocide unveiled the results of a research project that evaluated President Obama's choice to refrain from intervening in the Syrian Civil War. Researchers drawing on a variety of different methodologies concluded that the period when intervention by the Obama administration could have made a positive difference in terms of saving lives was "vanishingly short or nonexistent."

C ritics blasted the report for "absolving" the Obama administration of blame. Implicit in criticism of the report was the belief that a forceful intervention must be the right policy response to horrific violence against civilians. Leon Wieseltier, a literary critic, told *Tablet* magazine "If I had the time, I would gin up a parody of this [report] that will give us the computational-modeling algorithmic counterfactual analysis of John J. McCloy's decision not to bomb the Auschwitz ovens in 1944." U.S. Holocaust Museum officials, apparently bending to criticism, took the research down from its site.

The Holocaust Museum case highlights the importance of our seemingly recondite point. Abhorrence of entertaining counterfactuals forced the retraction of a report that might have led to a better understanding of when such interventions worked. Both scholarship and the recent historical record offer examples of interventions in active conflicts that lessened suffering— and others that heightened it. If we do not train a corps of students to confront these assessments, we (and, more importantly, the victims of violence and potential recipients of intervention) risk being governed by a corps of policy makers who will exacerbate crises with well-intentioned but ill-advised actions. Policy makers drawing on the "toolbox" metaphor, for instance, may view past cases as providing clear instructions for matching a set menu of policy options to urgent, time-sensitive problems, instead of viewing both the menu of policy options and problems like genocide as the complex outcomes of multi-stage, multi-actor processes. Instead of seriously evaluating the difficult calculus of death that the counterfactual entails, they may instead turn to policy-by-analogy, arguing that if, for example, targeted sanctions or military intervention were possible levers in one case, governments ought to pull them in other, similar cases.

We suggest two strategies for addressing students' ethical concerns: focusing on unintended consequences and assessing the intentions of actors making intervention decisions. First, introducing students to scholarship and literature that analyzes the unintended consequences of intervention can be useful: if intervention actually heightens the effects of war—if more people die than would have before, if UN peacekeepers bring cholera with them, if interveners themselves commit human rights violations, or if rebel groups are more likely to target civilians if peacekeepers are on the ground—then how should we understand the effects of those operations?

There is a substantial, careful body of scholarship on these unintended consequences—for example, Séverine Autesserre's *The Trouble with the Congo: Local Violence and the Failure of International Peacebuilding* and Alan J. Kuperman's "The Moral Hazard of Humanitarian Intervention: Lessons from the Balkans" both highlight how even well-intentioned interveners can make bad situations worse. Narrative non-fiction can also help students weigh the potentially devastating consequences of intervention— reading Jonathan Katz's *The Big Truck that Went By*, for example, can offer students a fine-grained understanding of the costs of intervention in Haiti. These texts can help students learn to weigh the costs of intervention and grasp how actions undertaken to stop bloodshed and suffering may prove unwise. Debating these unintended consequences can help foster an intellectual atmosphere that does not equate reasoned investigation of the counterfactual with an endorsement of "bystanderism."

Another tactic for helping students address difficult counterfactuals could involve sustained attention to familiar figures across a semester, with a focus on assessing their intentions. Coincidentally, Samantha Power presents educators with an important opportunity, since students can observe Power as an activist and as a policy maker. Students today can compare Power's arguments in *A Problem from Hell*, which argued that the United States failed to intervene and halt genocides in the 1990s because it simply did not want to, with her work as the UN ambassador representing the United States during a period when the Syrian war racked up an astounding number of civilian casualties. News clips and footage of Power's Security Council statements on Syria can help students retroactively unpack arguments about how the national interest, humanitarian goals, and intervention possibilities are constructed in different cases. This moves students from the idea that intervention failures are simply a matter of not caring enough (surely, having first read *A Problem from Hell*, they understand that Power cared enough) to the idea that assessing intervention outcomes requires recognizing that military intervention is an insufficient tool to halt humanitarian suffering in some cases. This focus on intentions can lead students back to carefully considering the counterfactual: would following Power's policy recommendations in *A Problem from Hell* have lessened Syrian suffering?

There are also methodological concerns. Counterfactual reasoning about interventions can also be difficult to teach because of methodological problems familiar to all social scientists. Efforts to understand intervention must contend with both fundamental problems of casual inference and a selection problem: that interventions are not randomly distributed. Cases that receive interventions are systematically different from cases that do not receive interventions.

The most rigorous way to assess whether peacekeeping (or any other form of intervention) "worked" would be to assign such interventions to conflicts at random. That is neither how the world works nor how any but the most amoral methodologist would want it to. Scholars have attempted a full range of sophisticated statistical methods to address this difficulty, but few are as intuitive for undergraduates to understand as matching techniques, particularly when paired with comparative case analysis. Because most undergraduates arrive in social science classes with a basic understanding of the scientific method but literally no understanding of statistics, the logic of paired comparison that underlies both strategies of study is immediately understandable in ways that other modeling strategies are not. Students can learn to ask and answer questions about which cases are most similar and which are most different, what the divergence in outcomes between these cases is, and, accordingly, to theorize about counterfactual intervention outcomes in real-world terms. In our own classrooms, for example, pairing instruction of Michael Gilligan and Ernesto Sergenti's "Do U.N. Interventions Cause Peace? Using Matching to Improve Causal Inference" with comparative case research assignments has helped students grasp the interrelated challenges that make assessing interventions difficult.

Another strategy might involve building real-time process evidence into course design. The instructor would identify one or two real-world, ongoing cases of atrocity or mass violence at the beginning of the semester and build time into each class session to discuss them. Drawing on journalistic and audiovisual evidence (Security Council meetings, news clips, etc.), students would be asked to summarize how competing arguments from theoretical accounts covered in course materials would interpret unfolding events. Students would ascribe how confident a given theory would be in making each prediction and how much the falsification of a given prediction would weaken their confidence in that theory. Even though much about any given situation will remain unobservable, theories usually make broad claims about the observable implications of different causal mechanisms. Systematically collecting and evaluating this evidence in real time would, of course, mimic what intelligence analysts, policy makers, and implementers must do themselves. It would also prove congruent with contemporary Bayesian approaches to process tracing. Extensions of this activity might involve separating students into different groups, asking them to evaluate using the same evidence using the same theories, and then comparing how each group's conclusions match (or fail to match) each others' findings.

Finally, there are epistemological concerns. The unknowability of counterfactual outcomes in devastating circumstances can be difficult for students to accept. Instructors can help students to normalize uncertainty by showing them how experts grapple with these problems. The most important lesson we can convey is how to convey how we know what we do not know. As scholars, therefore, it is especially appropriate for us to use our expertise to demonstrate what "not knowing" looks like. Sometimes, that may mean saying that we are very sure of some claim, but that there are alternatives that might also be probable; sometimes, it may mean admitting that despite careful study we cannot distinguish between competing causal claims, even if we can confidently reject others.

Instructors can share examples of scholarly disagreement and acceptance of uncertainty. For instance, in 2014, the TRIP survey of approximately 1,300 experts asked respondents to explicitly evaluate two major counterfactuals: "Would ISIS be as powerful as it is today if the United States had bombed Syrian government forces in the summer of 2013?" and "Would ISIS be as powerful as it is today if the United States had begun aggressively arming more secular elements of the Syrian rebellion (e.g., the Free Syrian Army) in the summer of 2013?" Expert opinion was indeterminate. On whether U.S. bombing would have weakened rebel strength, nearly as many experts said they did not know as replied "yes" or "no"; even 50 percent of specialists in human rights said they did not know. Similarly, "I don't know" was the most common answer for scholars in most international relations subfields to the question on arming secular Syrian rebels.

Presenting responsible uncertainty does not undermine our authority. Instead, it demonstrates that not every problem is amenable to "hot takes" or sloganeering. We can explicitly model for students how to evaluate the sorts of knowledge-claims that they will encounter outside our classrooms— in TED talks, in state of the union addresses, and on protest signs. Daniel Drezner writes of how the "ideas industry" in the early twenty-first century favors "thought leaders" who can confidently profess a given theory of change and fit it to any situation. He argues for a resurgence in criticism to help temper thought leaders' confidence and to poke holes in shoddy arguments. Helping students to see the difference between grounded and responsible criticism and simplistic knee-jerk rejection would be, in itself, a major contribution to their critical thinking skills.

Instructors could address such uncertainty through exercises like a research assignment that involves gathering policy recommendations about how to address historical cases made in real time by think tanks, nongovernmental organizations, and international organizations, and comparing their recommendations and predicted outcomes against actual intervention outcomes. Such an exercise would allow students to wrestle with unknowability while also developing both case expertise and a fine-grained understanding of what interventions look like in practice.

TEACHING PEACE AND WAR

K arl Marx castigated thinkers who "have hitherto only interpreted the world in various ways" when, he claimed, "the point is to change it." In our experience, many students interested in studying intervention, no matter their politics, would agree with him. Yet social scientists face an insuperable dilemma on those terms: changing the world requires some interpretation of it, but our interpretation of the world requires making claims about the unknowable—how some alternative world would have turned out. Assessing interventions into conflict or mass atrocity situations presents both scholars and policy makers with their worst-case scenario: situations in which even the best-case scenario involves loss of life, and in which the fundamental problem of casual inference combines unknowable outcomes with unthinkable horrors. Worse, such counterfactuals involve recognizing uncertainty when students—and we—crave confidence. Because complex, internationalized civil wars are (thankfully) rare, experts must draw on a limited set of somewhat contradictory cases to make claims, weakening their confidence in their judgments and leaving the field open for policy and norm entrepreneurs less troubled by ambiguity.

Social scientists training the next generation of policy makers, activists, and citizens should confront the challenges of making the classroom safe for doubt. We should help students see that accepting uncertainty does not imply accepting despair or helplessness. We can model how disciplined thinking can help avoid the sorts of errors that result from laziness, zealotry, or hubris. By helping students see the world as complicated, and helping them master tools to grapple with that complexity, we believe that instructors teaching the politics of intervention can help students arrive at a mature recognition of the limits of knowledge while helping them secure a sounder footing from which to make decisions.

ACKNOWLEDGMENTS

We are grateful to Daniel Solomon for his comments on a previous draft. All errors are our own.

RECOMMENDED READINGS

Autesserre, Séverine. 2012. "Dangerous Tales: Dominant Narratives on the Congo and Their Unintended Consequences." *African Affairs* 111. doi:10.1093/afraf/adr080

Autesserre, Séverine. 2010. *The Trouble with the Congo: Local Violence and the Failure of International Peacebuilding.* Cambridge: Cambridge University Press.

Bennett, Andrew. 2014. "Disciplining our Conjectures: Systematizing Process Tracing with Bayesian Analysis," in Andrew Bennett and Jeffrey Checkel (eds.), *Process Tracing: From Metaphor to Analytic Tool.* Cambridge: Cambridge University Press.

Drezner, Daniel. 2017. *The Ideas Industry: How Pessimists, Partisans, and Plutocrats are Transforming the Marketplace of Ideas.* Oxford: Oxford University Press.

Gilligan, Michael J., and Ernest J. Sergenti. 2008. "Do U.N. Interventions Cause Peace? Using Matching to Improve Causal Inference." *Quarterly Journal of Political Science* 3. doi:10.1561/100.00007051

Katz, Jonathan M. 2013. *The Big Truck That Went By: How the World Came to Save Haiti and Left Behind a Disaster.* New York: Palgrave Macmillan.

Kuperman, Alan J. 2008. "The Moral Hazard of Humanitarian Intervention: Lessons from the Balkans." *International Studies Quarterly* 52. doi:10.1111/j.1468-2478.2007.00491.x

Marx, Karl. "Theses On Feuerbach." Available at <https://www.marxists.org/archive/marx/works/1845/theses/>, last accessed October 15, 2017.

Power, Samantha. 2002. *A Problem from Hell: America and the Age of Genocide.* New York: Harper Collins.

Singal, Jesse. 2017. "Here Is the Syria Report Withdrawn by the U.S. Holocaust Museum." Available at <http://nymag.com/daily/intelligencer/2017/09/here-is-the-holocaust-museum-syria-report.html>, last accessed November 28, 2017.

"TRIP Snap Poll III: Seven Questions on Current Global Issues for International Relations Scholars." 2015. vailable at <https://trip.wm.edu/reports/2014/2015Snap.pdf>, last accessed October 15, 2017.

Truth, Sources, and the Fog of War

JOAKIM BERNDTSSON ⓘ AND ARNE F. WACKENHUT ⓘ

Teaching and learning about war is inherently difficult. Both students and teachers experience varying levels of frustration and unease when confronted with accounts of violence and death. Yet most teachers in International Relations (IR), Peace or War Studies, and related fields would agree that learning about the "realities of war" is important for many reasons. We want our students to discuss and reflect on the nature of violence, on moral issues of right and wrong, the effects of war on societies and individuals, on the possibilities of preventing or ending wars and, more broadly, on issues of truth and justice.

The challenge, of course, is to design learning activities that engage and activate students while at the same time making room for discussions about the emotional aspects of studying war and violence. In early 2013, we were pondering these issues, seeking to devise new teaching and learning activities on the realities of war for students in the undergraduate IR program at the School of Global Studies, University of Gothenburg. How would we go about introducing this important but challenging topic to students at an early stage of the program? How could we inspire critical discussion and reflection while, at the same time, training them as analysts?

The following describes and reflects on an exercise we designed to address some of these issues. Through the assignment, students are confronted with narratives of violence in war, but they are also tasked with assessing and analyzing sources, and reflecting on issues of truth and deception. Thus, we provide one example of a teaching and learning activity that aims to introduce a difficult and sensitive topic while, at the same time, providing an opportunity for students to develop key academic skills such as source criticism, data collection, reflective and critical thinking, as well as academic writing. The essay proceeds as follows: First, we briefly describe the background of the exercise and introduce the pedagogical rationale underlying our decision to adopt a combination of guided discovery and problem-based learning. In the following part, we describe the assignment in more detail, before providing an aggregation of reflections and experiences from both teachers and students who have participated in the exercise. Last, in a concluding section, we flesh out some of the more general implications of problem-based learning activities as well as some ideas for future development of this and similar exercises.

The idea for this exercise came to one of us after re-reading the novel *In the Lake of the Woods* by American author and Vietnam veteran Tim O'Brien. Eventually, the book provided both the theme and the case for this assignment. Those familiar with O'Brien's work will know that he constantly invites his readers to reflect on questions of truth, reality, and the nature of storytelling, but also on moral issues of war and violence more broadly. Essentially, this was what we wanted our students to do. In addition, we wanted a case for the exercise that was not only relevant but also well documented.

In O'Brien's novel, the main character, John Wade, has recurring flashbacks from his time in Vietnam, many of which relate to the massacre at My Lai or "Pinkville" on March 16, 1968. Even though nearly 50 years have passed, the tragic case of My Lai remains very relevant for students of war and violence—not least because it continues to raise challenging questions about war crimes, responsibility, and accountability in armed conflict. Moreover, there is a wealth of publicly available information on My Lai, including tens of thousands of pages of official inquiries and court records, decades of scholarly work, documentaries, and media reports. Finally, and in spite of these vast amounts of both data and research, many questions about the events that occurred in March 1968 remain essentially unanswered.

Hence, My Lai provides a suitable basis for learning activities that combine the larger issues of war and violence with more concrete tasks of collecting and assessing different types and sources of data. With these considerations in the background, we went about designing a group assignment for our first-year students. Before describing this in more detail, however, some words on the pedagogical rationale for the exercise are in order.

Over the last decade or so, pedagogical research has increasingly shown that traditional forms of instruction, such as the ubiquitous lecture format, are not always ideally suited to facilitate student learning. Oftentimes, "what the teacher does" is less important than "what the student does" to achieve intended learning outcomes. This realization has led to the emergence of a number of nontraditional forms of instruction that put a stronger emphasis on the students and seek to empower them by enabling them to take control of their own learning processes.

Drawing on these findings, the My Lai exercise is—pedagogically speaking—inspired by a combination of guided discovery learning on the one hand, and problem-based learning, which is commonly used in the medical sciences, on the other. The amalgamation of these approaches, both of which involve confronting students with complex phenomena, is intended to create a stimulating learning environment in which the students not only learn together—in groups of five to seven students—but also learn from each other in discussions and debates. Moreover, students learn through practicing skills, in this case by collecting and assessing sources of data on a specific topic. Teachers mostly function as facilitators in this context—providing support when and where needed but, at the same time, making it clear that students, individually and collectively, are the driving force in the learning and knowledge creation process.

As mentioned above, our exercise is part of an introductory course in IR (with around 80 students in total). Apart from key theories and concepts, the course includes a number of teaching and learning activities designed to help students develop academic writing and referencing skills. The My Lai assignment is a part of these activities and is specifically designed to train students in what historians refer to as "source criticism" or "source analysis"—a set of tools designed to help us assess the reliability of information and sources.

Before introducing the actual assignment, we give a short (45 minutes) lecture that is intended to equip students with the necessary tools to analyze and assess sources with regard to their authenticity, their distance in time to the events described, their independence, as well as potential biases. Following the lecture, the students are given a hand-out and asked to read two very different accounts of the events that occurred in My Lai. Importantly we as teachers have not yet mentioned the case as such—the students are simply given the information that they will be working on in smaller groups of about five students to practice their source criticism skills by analyzing a historical case. They are also told that the case, and the accounts they are about to read, deal with excessive use of violence, and they are encouraged to use their groups to talk about their feelings about the case.

Confronting students with graphic descriptions of violence requires careful planning and reflection. As teachers in higher education, we should not shy away from difficult or sensitive topics, but we also need to be aware of the potential consequences for students. We want students to engage emotionally with the subject, but we also want to avoid situations where students feel they cannot talk about their feelings or reactions with teachers or fellow students. We have chosen to work with a historical case to create a distance between the students and the events described. We also identify the subject of the two accounts as sensitive and we suggest a forum for discussing negative emotional reactions. Thus, we seek to convey the message that negative feelings are both common and normal and we encourage students to reflect on this aspect of the assignment.

The two accounts consist of the official Combat Action Report filed by Lt. Col. Frank A. Barker, Jr., and the letter to Congress and the Pentagon by Ronald L. Ridenhour. Barker's Combat Action Report represents a highly technical account of the incident, presenting the operation in bureaucratic/military language as "well planned, well executed and successful," and provides details of 128 killed and 11 captured enemy combatants. In stark contrast, Ridenhour's letter—based on his conversations with several people who were in My Lai or "Pinkville" on that day—quite graphically recounts how troops assigned to Task Force Barker indiscriminately shot and killed several hundred civilians. The letter by Ridenhour also describes in detail the actions of Lt. William Calley—the only person to be tried and convicted for crimes committed in My Lai.

Having read these accounts in class, there is usually—and quite understandably so—some tension in the classroom. In this situation, the students are asked for their spontaneous reactions. As the case of My Lai is not well known among Swedish students, their reactions are usually a mixture of both surprise and indignation. There is also a feeling of frustration upon having read two conflicting accounts of the events. What is true and what is false? What really happened at My Lai? Who was to blame? At this point, the students are usually very keen to learn more about the case, and we try to use this momentum when introducing the exercise.

The working groups are expected—using the tools of source criticism—to analyze both documents they have just received as well any other primary and secondary source they can find to address three questions: First: How do you assess the reliability of the two documents? Why are they reliable or unreliable? Second: How many combatants and non-combatants—if any—were killed during the incident that took place on March 16, 1968? What casualty figures exist, and how do you assess their reliability? Third: Who—if anyone—gave the order to attack civilians? How do you assess the reliability of this information? The working groups are given ten days to try to answer the questions and write a six- to seven-page report. Upon completion, two to three working groups are put together in seminar groups to present their findings and to give feedback on each other's work.

As anyone familiar with the case of My Lai will know, the first question is challenging, while the following two questions are formidably difficult to answer. At this point, however, most of the students are unaware of this. As they try to work their way through thousands of pages of official documents, scholarly work, and hours of documentaries, their frustration at not being able to find definitive answers will mount, again forming an important part of the exercise.

During the course of the exercise, the teachers are available to the working groups, but there is no structured supervision or intervention—the groups are mostly left to work on their own. At the end of the ten days, the groups submit their reports and prepare for the seminar by reading the reports of one or two other working groups. To guide their reading, the groups are asked to assess each other's work in terms of strengths and areas that could be improved on. Furthermore, they are encouraged to reflect on differences between the reports and the answers provided by other groups. Additionally, each group writes a short logbook entry (200–250 words) on the course website. In these entries, which are only accessible to teachers, the groups are asked to collectively reflect on the exercise and the work in the group. These short texts serve the purpose of providing a forum for reflection on the case, their learning processes, and to help students prepare for the seminars.

At the seminars, the groups give a short oral presentation of their findings and then move on to discuss each other's work. In these discussions, it becomes clear that not only have groups used different sources and therefore arrived at different answers to the questions, but also that they may have made different assessments of the same sources. This collective experience adds to student learning by underlining the difficulties of arriving at a single and "true" narrative of what occurred at My Lai (and thus in any other situation like it). It also shows the importance of rigor, transparency, and critical self-reflection throughout the entire research process.

Since the autumn of 2013, some 600 students have completed the assignment. Student feedback has been systematically collected through logbook entries, seminar discussions, and course evaluations. This means that we now have a fairly good idea of their experiences and concerns. It is clear that, for a majority of students, the exercise works well in terms of training analytical skills. Although most students have worked with source criticism before coming to the university, they generally agree that these skills need continuous development and practice.

In student evaluations, it is also clear that working together on a real-world case as well as discussing sources, information, and issues of truth and deception in smaller groups and at seminars, have contributed to their learning. Of course, not all students have found the exercise interesting or useful. Some have pointed out that they already know about source criticism, while others found the collective aspects of the exercise challenging. As teachers, we have responded to this criticism by emphasizing the need for continuous practice and by explaining even more carefully how analytical skills and critical reflection can be developed through peer-assisted and problem-based learning.

Working with the My Lai case inevitably involves being confronted with explicit and sometimes disturbing images of war and violence in the form of, for instance, witness accounts or images available online. In their written feedback as well as in discussions, students have sometimes described their reactions to this part of the exercise. They occasionally noted how it made them feel angry, sad, or frustrated. In addition, this encounter with the realities of war and violence—albeit through a historical case—has been described by many students as lending a sense of importance to the exercise as well as making their studies in IR more concrete. As university teachers, we need to be able to explain why this should be part of their learning but, also, be ready to give advice and support to students who find it distressing. In our experience, encouraging students to discuss their reactions and experiences has worked well. We might, however, want to consider even more careful measures to ensure that students who might have witnessed or even experienced traumatic events similar to the My Lai massacre have a chance to prepare themselves or take other appropriate measures.

Also, taking note of relatively recent research on constructive controversy we might also want to consider modifying the instructions for the seminar in which the different project groups present their findings. By forcing, or at least encouraging, the larger seminar groups to arrive at a consensus with regard to the three questions guiding the assignment, we could stimulate their learning processes even further since this would help them engage even more closely with the subject matter at hand.

In sum, our experience of this combination of guided discovery and problem-based learning has worked well for both students and teachers. We think it can be used to great effect in IR and related fields, as it can help students fulfill a number of different expected learning outcomes in the confines of one larger teaching and learning activity. We are certainly not arguing that this particular type of assignment should completely replace other activities, like the traditional lecture, but that it should be regarded a valuable complement to the teachers' toolbox of teaching and learning activities designed to aid students in their learning processes.

In the specific context of our undergraduate program in IR, My Lai represented a useful case to achieve the learning objectives, that is, help students learn about the realities and fog of war, while at the same time helping them improve key skills in academic writing, reference management, and, not least, source criticism and analysis. Especially the last skill deserves particular attention and emphasis in a time where "alternative facts," "fake news," and large-scale active measures and influence campaigns force us to critically reflect on information we encounter in terms of its validity and veracity. Thus, source criticism is becoming an essential skill not only for undergraduate students in IR and related fields, but for all of us as responsible citizens.

ACKNOWLEDGEMENTS

The authors wish to thank Elizabeth Olsson for invaluable comments on this essay.

ORCID

Joakim Berndtsson ⓘ http://orcid.org/0000-0003-1352-1158
Arne F. Wackenhut ⓘ http://orcid.org/0000-0001-5509-6132

RECOMMENDED READINGS

Johnson, David W., and Roger T. Johnson. 2009. "Energizing Learning: The Instructional Power of Conflict." *Educational Researcher* 38 (1): 37–51. doi:10.3102/0013189X 08330540.

Olson, James S., and Randy Roberts. 1998. *My Lai: A Brief History with Documents*. New York: Bedford Books.

Rankin, Jocelyn. 1998. *Handbook on Problem-Based Learning*. New York: Medical Library Association.

Conflict and Engagement in "Reacting to the Past" Pedagogy

JULIE C. TATLOCK AND PAULA REITER

Reacting to the Past (RTTP) is an established program that works to engage students on a deeper level by having them work with primary materials actively through role playing. We used an established French Revolution game tweaked for our particular student population. Generally set in historical moments of extreme conflict and debate, the games are meant to be a catalyst for student learning and engagement. In RTTP pedagogy, students are assigned primary readings from the era under discussion and are then given a role to play in an interactive game. For the French Revolution, for example, a student might be assigned the role of a literary figure, a politician, or an artist. The game is intended to take about six weeks, leaving ten weeks for lecture and reading. Using the primary readings as their guide, students react to arguments and discussions based on their characters' interpretations of events. The program has an established curriculum and hosts conferences where instructors learn how to manage the games successfully. Hosted by Barnard College with games published by Norton, RTTP has an impressive record of success.

We chose this pedagogy specifically to enhance creative and experiential learning in our humanities course. Mount Mary University is a women's school that blends a liberal arts education with career preparation. Our students come from extremely diverse backgrounds and have just as varied educational preparation. As educators we wanted a course that would not only explore humanities topics but also help our students hone skills in areas of argumentation and public speaking, but also in more hidden skills like negotiation, empathy, critical listening, and building confidence, all of which are necessary in handling any conflict. To achieve our specific goals we slowed down the course of the game rather dramatically so that we could build in assignments to reach our learning objectives, which can be found below.

On a basic level, we wanted students to read, understand, and discuss Romantic writers and gain foundational knowledge of key places, events, and ideas of the Revolutionary era. Students worked to develop skills in public speaking, both prepared and impromptu, and to write effective speeches and papers to persuade an imagined historic audience. While maintaining historically accurate character positions, students explored historical perspectives and developed empathy and understanding for ideas and values that may not have been their own. Finally, students engaged in compromise and negotiation to reach team goals. Ultimately the combined course objects led students to a close analysis of historical causation.

What we found was that this type of learning drastically improved student participation, which we expected, but it also took the women in the class outside of their comfort zones and forced them to actively confront intense conflicts. They had to imagine themselves in the historical period, reacting to events as historical figures. Students navigated the complexity of historical arguments and debates, not only exploring the facts, but also the ways people of the time interpreted and used facts to make decisions. Students opened their minds to ideas that were, and perhaps remain, controversial. They learned to argue with each other in a nuanced and respectful way.

How does this method impact student learning? While we have only one class to draw on, initial data suggest vastly improved student engagement. For example, attendance in this course was nearly perfect. Students attended, on average, 98.7 percent of class time. Only one student missed over a single day of class, and she missed two days of class to attend a conference. Additionally, the rate of completion for assignments was also exceptionally high. The class average for reading quizzes was just over 98 percent, and the rate of on time submission for homework assignments was 92.6 percent. Not surprisingly, with excellent daily work, students earned much higher final grades as well. The average final grade was a 94.7 percent.

It is handy to have numbers to quantify student engagement and achievement, and to support our experience of how students responded to this class, but our experiences with the students are even more powerful than the numbers suggest. Anecdotally, students told us that this class was by far the most exciting and engaging course they were taking. Students regularly came early and stayed after class to continue working. Even on the day of the final exam, students did not want to leave the class. Outside of class, students became friends and joked about calling each other their character's names, so absorbed in the game that they began to think of each other by their class names. Perhaps most importantly, students applied what they were learning about the French Revolution to what they were seeing in modern social, political, and economic spheres. They often mentioned that the class taught them how difficult it could be to come to rational decisions when tensions were running high and violence loomed. They found it really frustrating when a well-reasoned and well-argued debate lost to outpourings of irrational and passionate feelings.

The first major assignment in this course asks students to introduce themselves, in character, to the rest of the class. To prepare, we spend time in class discussing rhetorical strategies, paying particular attention to how class and gender can be asserted, maintained, and revealed through language. Students receive a packet outlining their character's political views, economic goals, family ties, religious views, and a host of other details. The challenge for students is to integrate all this information into a believable, sympathetic, fully realized character. There are no easy villains or flat characters in the game. Each student must remain faithful to her character's personal background when forming a response to an issue. For example, a character may have hidden financial anxieties that shape his response to a vote on confiscating church lands. Another character may have family ties to a vulnerable citizen who could be damaged by a move to extend political representation. Others may have financial ties to the plantations in Saint-Domingue that contribute to their views on citizenship for free blacks and slaves.

Mastering three of the key learning objectives for the course (to explore historical perspectives and develop an empathy and understanding for perspectives and values that may not be your own; to write effective speeches; to develop skills in public speaking), begins with this assignment asking students to introduce their characters. What students develop over the semester is full understanding of how a particular, complicated human receives political information and responds to it. Every character in the game reads or hears about the theories of Locke, Voltaire, and Rousseau. Yet how each character uses, reads, and misreads these theories differs tremendously. Students find that the same quote from Rousseau can be used by characters on opposite sides of an issue. Students are amazed and ask themselves, how can this be?

This character building was integral to how students shaped their arguments and it allowed them to engage fully in heated arguments without feeling personally attacked. They learned that to be successful in changing the course of a debate or to change the nature of the conflict, they needed to operate from a strong base of knowledge. It was necessary to know the intricacies of their own character and the others in the game. It was invaluable to be able to deftly use the primary documents to build a rational argument, but they also needed those softer skills mentioned earlier. They had to speak to the personal desires of other characters, to know who could be persuaded and who they did not want to anger. Students worked to choose carefully what they said publicly and what they said privately, often making quiet background deals to achieve an objective. Perhaps most impactful were the times when words ultimately failed and violence won the day, when conflict turned to war.

Students quickly become frustrated when what seemed like an easy issue turns out to be infinitely more complicated. Each issue that gets debated, whether large or small, is connected by a partially invisible web of personal and political goals and prejudices. Nothing, it turns out, is straight forward. And yet, votes must be cast and decisions must be made. The compromises needed to move forward on an issue and the pressures of time, finances, and threatened violence left students feeling only partially satisfied with any decision. These difficulties only intensify as the game draws closer to the ultimate decision (to go to war or not). When unforeseen circumstances beyond their control derailed the work of many class periods, students had to regroup and nimbly change direction. Over the semester, students came to terms with the realities of political decision making. It is messy and convoluted. It requires a great deal of compromise, and no side is ever fully satisfied.

One issue of intense debate for our class was the political representation of women. Because we teach at a women's college, we were particularly interested in how the major concepts and texts of the Enlightenment and the French Revolution would be applied to women. Where do women fit into Rousseau's social contract? Did the *Declaration of Rights of Man and Citizen* include women? What does it mean to be an active or a passive citizen? We needed to think quite creatively about how to have a group of women have and show historical empathy for men who believed in strict patriarchal values and "separate spheres." This was also a unique moment in the game as nearly all of the characters generally agreed that women were not equal to men and should not have roles in politics. Here the conflict was between the women and men they portrayed.

S tudents debated these complex questions during a special class session called the Etta Palm Salon. Etta Palm was a wealthy, elite feminist who hosted a salon for the glittering intellectuals of the day. Originally Dutch, Palm moved to Paris and is best known for her address *Discourse on the Injustice of the Laws in Favour of Men at the Expense of Women*. We asked our dean to play the role of Etta Palm, and her training as a philosopher made the session particularly successful. As Palm explained her feminist position, our students had to respond in character. What Palm proposed seemed so trifling and obvious in our own historical moment, but taking into consideration a distant time, place, and culture, the students had to put forward arguments that men would have made against extending the *Declaration of Human Rights* to women.

It was quite an amazing thing to hear the incredibly articulate arguments our women made against women having power. It may have been some of the best argumentation of the semester, perhaps because of the inherent conflict the students felt in what they understood to be true versus what they were forced to argue. It was also a true moment for historical empathy and lent itself to a discussion of how, in a conflict, you can find a way to understand the opposition's point of view. In the end, the vote was not even close. Women would not be granted equality before the law or political representation.

Like the woman question, the situation in Saint-Domingue further complicated questions about human rights, private property, the uses of violence, and how to finance a government. Just at the moment the students were arguing about equality in the French Assembly, a massive slave revolt occurs on French-owned Saint-Domingue. Not all of our characters agreed in this debate. There were one or two lone voices, the people who were "ahead of their time," when it came to slavery. How could the assertion that men are born and remain free and equal be reconciled with the declaration that property in all forms is an inviolable and sacred right? When philosophical ideals come crashing into financial necessities and prejudice, who wins?

By now, students had become experts in collaborating with classmates, negotiating with rival factions, and devising and presenting logical arguments supported by evidence. The debate over extending rights to free black men and male slaves in Saint-Domingue came at the end of the semester and brought together all their leadership, rhetorical, and textual knowledge. Students had to devise a plan with satisfactory philosophical, political, and financial outcomes. The financial demands to keep sugar profits flowing into the otherwise depleted French coffers had to be met or they would not be able to finance the government and army and stave off foreign invasion. But how could that be accomplished if slaves were recognized as having rights? Students also had to contend with potential foreign conflicts. How would the United States feel about the abolition of slavery in a region so close to its own slave states? What about countries who still made significant sums of money from the slave trade? Would they see this as the first salvo in an attack the entire trade in people? Students explored several plans, including immediate emancipation, gradual emancipation, and the idea of compensating slave owners for financial losses. It was at this moment of heated debate that France was invaded by outside powers, a situation that turned the Assembly to more immediate military arrangements.

There are several reasons why this pedagogy was successful in both building student skills and as a meaningful way of teaching about conflict. Active learning is memorable. It engages students on multiple levels and makes learning personal. Students were fully invested in their characters. They wanted their characters to win the game and take the day. The various conflicts of the French Revolution became their conflicts. The passion of their characters became their passions. This motivated them to go above and

beyond in learning the content, engaging the resources, and actively participating in classes. In this case, we took a moment of immense human conflict
and forced students to develop historical understanding, historical empathy,
and the skills needed to navigate complex situations. The impact, we think,
is huge! When students who took this course now engage conflicts in the real
world, they have a skill set to handle things appropriately. They can now look
at war and peace in a world context with a much more nuanced outlook about
the nature of human disagreement. What could be more important given the
world in which we live?

Group Projects as Conflict Management Pedagogy

AMANDA ELLSWORTH DONAHOE

Conflict Resolution as a field has wrestled with the tensions between practice and theory. My course, introducing the field to undergraduates, shares this struggle—or it did until I reconfigured an assignment called the Conflict Map for teaching conflict management by using small groups. Based on Paul Wehr's 1979 book, *Conflict Regulation*, the Conflict Map is a research paper that requires students to analyze a current case of conflict by researching its component parts and then assessing conflict regulation potential. When assigned individually to students, this assignment does not bridge the gap between theory and practice. As a group project, however, the assignment requires students to navigate personal conflict within their groups while applying theory and practical skills from the course to their shared case. Groups are a natural and appropriate source of conflict from which students can learn because their participation is driven by personal goals for success that may potentially be hindered by their reliance on the participation of group mates.

S tudents refer to this assignment as "meta" because of the way that both the content of the assignment and the interaction of the groups reflect on the goals of the course and require the application of its content. This personal engagement combined with interdependence forces students to consistently reflect on the ways in which the conflict management skills they are learning in the course are practical both in their daily lives and in their collaborative research. Further, learning these skills as a group works to empower members to hold each other accountable to lessons learned about managing group tensions constructively. Students learn conflict resolution by resolving group conflict. Recognizing that these skills are effective creates a positive feedback loop that reinforces the value of these skills in their lives.

The benefits of collaborative learning, such as group projects, are numerous. Carol Colbeck, Susan Campbell, and Stefani Bjorklund argued in 2000 that collaborative learning leads to improved communication, problem solving, and—valuable for our purposes—conflict management. David

Johnson, Roger Johnson, and Karl Smith previously pointed out that conflict management skills must be taught as part of the group process in order for collaborative learning to be most effective. Their larger argument is that collaborative learning must be deliberate and purposeful, and that simply grouping students together for an assignment is not enough to foster collaborative learning. At the same time, Larry Michaelsen, L. Dee Fink, and Arletta Knight suggested that collaborative tasks should compel high levels of individual accountability, group interaction and discussion, and meaningful feedback for group members, in addition to explicit rewards or payoffs for successful group accomplishment. In what follows, I describe the Conflict Map Group Project, the way that it meets these requirements, and discuss the ways in which this assignment is a successful pedagogy for teaching conflict management.

Undergraduate students rarely cheer when presented with a group project, particularly when their grade is tied to group success. They have likely had bad experiences on previous group assignments because they lacked the skills to manage the conflicts that arise in an academically high-stakes situation. This conflict situation is comparable to the various kinds of conflicts addressed in the course in which conflict resolution skills are so valuable. This means that the stakes for group projects have to be high enough to matter. The conflict map is a large (40 percent of final grade) research project. Students cannot succeed in the class without a viable group project. The class discusses the challenges of collaborative projects openly before being assigned to groups. This gives students space to express their concerns broadly without reflecting on classmates.

The actual grouping process is an important one. For this assignment, students rank their interests on a list of relevant real-world cases of conflict. Using student responses in concert with a "getting to know you" survey such as the one Barbara Oakley et al. provide, I assemble students into groups of no more than three or four. Small groups encourage greater individual accountability. Good groups require diverse levels of ability and should strive for diversity of voices and experience, but should avoid isolating at-risk students. Diversity will mean different things on different campuses/courses but one consideration may be grouping first or second year students with more advanced students. More experienced students benefit from teaching lessons learned in research, writing, and citations; and less experienced students provide energy and enthusiasm. Instructors should be aware that this dynamic can create problematic hierarchies. Achieving diversity is difficult early in the class, but a "Getting to Know You" survey will help. A final consideration when putting groups together should be student schedules and availability outside of class so that groups can meet together.

When topics and groups are announced, students move to sit in their new groups and the class revisits the discussion on their concerns regarding group projects. Groups are encouraged as their first collaborative act to co-author an agreement regarding their expectations for themselves and each other. Groups might agree to "work diligently to be prepared for meetings," or "communicate openly when they cannot meet deadlines." Expectation Agreements should be as realistic as possible, so students are encouraged to avoid commitments to "never miss a meeting," for example. This first activity works to assuage student concerns regarding working as a team. That they will be researching a case that is unique to their group will also contribute to a sense of group identity, which may contribute to cohesiveness as they move forward.

The first assigned task for the Conflict Map Group is to thoroughly read the assignment and write a proposal for dividing tasks among group members. Oakley et al. advise against the divide and conquer method of students parceling out pieces of the assignment as it fosters autonomy over interdependence. The Conflict Map, however, requires students to research components of a conflict that are purposefully deeply interconnected, such that even when researched separately, a successful final draft requires collaboration and synthesis of the components in the final analysis.

So, even when groups pursue the divide and conquer method, they are still engaging in a great deal of group interaction. Class time is used to compare and discuss these proposals across groups so that the instructor can engage and offer guidance to the process. Students then submit a proposal for their group's Plan of Action for approval allowing the instructor the opportunity to ensure fair allocation of responsibilities as well as adding a level of supervision in holding group members accountable during the project. Students usually agree to each take sections and work together on the final analysis sections with added responsibilities for writing the summary, editing, citations, and formatting/organizing a presentation.

The Conflict Map assignment is a very structured assignment with a strict fifteen-page limit (not including cover sheet or works cited), and the following required sections with detailed descriptions of required content: 1. Summary (one page); 2. Conflict History; 3. Conflict Context; 4. Conflict Parties; 5. Issues; 6. Dynamics; 7. Alternative Routes to Solution; and 8. Conflict Regulation Potential.

To ensure that all group members start with a comparable understanding of the case, all group members are required to write the Conflict History. A writing workshop is useful here in which group members exchange drafts and discuss content priorities. In this way, students are introduced to each other's writing as they establish a collective history draft. As group dynamics present themselves, instructors can draw parallels to examples from class.

Groups work to limit the remaining sections to two pages and struggle to decide what fits most appropriately in each section. For example, a group writing on South Sudan wrestled with whether Sudan was fully covered in History and Context or should be included as a secondary or interested third party. Groups critically assess and analyze the conflict in sections 7 and 8. These sections have a tendency to expand in later stages of writing as group members' understanding of the conflict develops. Groups respond to this by trying to reduce the length of previous sections. This deliberative process achieves high levels of interaction but it may also result in territoriality as space on the page becomes a valuable resource. The student who included Sudan as an interested third party resisted the group's decision to cut this section as a space-saving mechanism, but ultimately yielded to the claim that more room was needed for the final two sections of the paper. It would be evident later that this was not the right choice and that accommodating the group would not lead to success, but it is an example of students not yet having the skills to competently resolve conflict.

Skills such as listening, assertive communication, and recognition of conflict styles are taught using in-class activities provided by resources such as *The Conflict and Communication Activity Book*. For example, in "Right Listening," students rotate three roles: speaking, listening, and observing the listener. In this way, students think critically about how they listen from each perspective. They are encouraged and encourage each other to avoid interrupting, listen for both content and speaker's feelings, and remove distractions, including cell phones. In a paper on Afghanistan, students disagreed over terminology for the group known as the Islamic State of Iraq and the Levant. Following this exercise, students who had argued for using the commonly used acronym ISIS, listened more openly to the suggestion of peers that using Daesh, the group's Arabic acronym, better reflected the role that the group played in their case study. Practicing these skills in a structured and formal way with group mates prepared them for informal unstructured interactions in project work.

To learn assertive communication, groups identify a series of statements as either aggressive or nonassertive, and discuss what each style communicates. Groups then revise statements to be assertive. Recognizing each of these styles and collectively identifying why assertive statements are more effective provides individual members with the vocabulary to address these issues in communication with group members. For one group, a sophomore identified early that her own nonassertive communication style contributed to a dynamic in which her two group mates, both seniors, wrestled for leadership. This dynamic was more evident to her when students took a personal conflict style inventory.

The conflict style inventory, like the one available from the U.S. Institute of Peace, presents students with various conflict scenarios and asks students to choose behaviors that best exemplify how they would respond. Students who feel their results are accurate (this is generally the case) gain insight into patterns in their behaviors. As a class, students identify whether or not they think their results might change depending on the kinds of relationships they imagined as they took the survey. For example, students may be more likely to answer questions as a Competer if they are thinking about conflict with a sibling, as an Accommodator or Avoider if they are thinking about conflict with a boss, or as a Compromiser when interacting with a close friend. Although students may have strong tendencies toward a particular conflict style, each of these styles may be valuable in different settings and different relationship dynamics.

When students discussed which conflict styles they prefer to use as a group, the sophomore used assertive communication, to draw the seniors' attention to the fact that they were both acting like Competers and that perhaps more "compromising" behaviors were appropriate. Having this vocabulary available empowered her to address the problem, and her groupmates were responsive to her communication style. Throughout these activities, and others on bargaining, negotiation, and mediation, the overarching theme is that conflict is natural and has the potential to be constructive. There is going to be conflict within student groups. Understanding that this is the case and equipping students to deal with it in ways that are productive to the group gives them both conflict management tools and practice.

Students have bad experiences in group projects because they lack the skills to effectively resolve conflict. This is true, but it also fails to address the issue of poorly applied group assignments. While creating a high-stakes assignment is imperative to driving the group dynamic, creating a supportive learning environment is important for individual student success. Two processes created support scaffolding for this learning process: group assessment/peer evaluations, and drafts. Group assessment forms such as the ones provided by Oakley et al. are distributed early in the project to help members assess overall group health and to think critically about the way they are functioning collectively. Groups are asked: do meetings start on time, are all members prepared, does everyone listen and feel listened to? The first distribution of this form is useful in identifying potential patterns that may inhibit group success. For example, one group acknowledged collectively that they were not allocating enough time at meetings to achieve their tasks when none of the individual members had wanted to suggest that they meet either longer or more often. A follow-up assessment can be done later in the term when the instructor finds it most useful to refocus attention on constructive group dynamics.

Peer evaluation forms require students to evaluate each of their group mates. The evaluation categories include: attendance to meetings, participation, responsibilities, and contribution. Discussing these categories as a class familiarizes students with the process, but also reinforces the norms of individual accountability. These forms are also distributed two times over the course of the project, and again, the first evaluation is not handed in. Instead, group members discuss them together openly. This allows the group to address issues with each other directly. This interaction is relatively low pressure for two reasons. First, the forms are distributed early enough in the project that students are unlikely to be very frustrated with each other yet. Second, the instructor is not directly involved. This discussion serves to confirm group expectations and may allow groups to curb potential problems such as students not contributing or attending meetings. It also allows students the opportunity to reflect on their own behaviors and the way that they are perceived by group members.

The second distribution of peer evaluations are collected. Ideally, this is done before rough drafts are due in order for the instructor to intervene if necessary. Interventions can be done collectively or individually with particular students. This scaffolding of assessment and evaluation acts as a security measure for student success and it can provide opportunities for creative interventions that directly utilize the skills of the class. For example, it might be useful to organize a mediation with the group with either a neutral group member, or perhaps a student from another group as mediator. This again serves to reinforce the value of conflict resolution skills on a personal level.

The second layer of scaffolding is a rough draft deadline. Formal rough drafts (complete, fully edited) are due two weeks before the final draft. It is important that rough drafts be returned with thorough suggestions for improvement and in time for revision. The benefits of this process are many. Students are better able to meet expectations on the assignment when they are clear about what those expectations are and how to achieve them. Further, the instructor can hold students accountable to the group's Plan of Action. The drafting process acts as a safeguard so that no one member or even systemic group misunderstanding about the assignment can endanger the collective grade as long as group members are responsive to draft feedback.

For example, on the South Sudan paper, despite the need for space, Sudan clearly ought to be described as an interested party to the conflict and I noted this in draft feedback. The group was able to reassess their strategy and revise the paper to include necessary information before their choices had a negative impact on their shared final grade. This was also a valuable reminder that group thinking can result in detrimental strategies. In feedback, I asked group members to reflect on their earlier debate about Sudan, then we discussed alternative ways that the group could have addressed the issue to arrive at a different result. The absence/poor application of conflict resolution skills also served as a learning opportunity.

After final drafts have been submitted, groups present their projects to the class. Groups then meet a final time to reflect on their experience together using a debrief form that students fill out individually following the discussion. The form asks groups to think about their process, including: meetings, communication, decision making, deadlines, inclusion, and power dynamics. Groups are asked about the division of responsibilities, whether or not they were met, whether or not they were fair, and how they might have been allocated differently. Many students report that seeing the list of each members' responsibilities reminded them of how much their colleagues contributed and accomplished during the project.

Groups are also asked how disagreements were handled within the group and how students responded to tension. As groups talk through these issues, students are confronted with their own performance. Individual submissions give them the space to communicate elements of their group dynamic that they may not have been willing to communicate directly to members of their group, or that the instructor may not have already been aware of. It also gives them time to consider their experiences autonomously. Their final debriefs exhibit a great deal of self-awareness as a result. One student acknowledged that, "Truthfully, many of the problems that were brought up were most likely caused by me."

The final set of questions help students identify what went well, whether or not students are pleased with the group's performance overall, and finally, how their experiences were affected by membership in the class. A small sample of their responses evidence the degree to which they practiced and internalized the lessons and tools of the class: "[W]hen conflict does pop up, I learned that it's best to address it directly and politely, even when it feels awkward to do so. I think we all had class material in the back of our minds. As a result, we definitely displayed more restraint than I have seen in other group projects when tensions rise. I do not think that the group would have developed the same collaborative framework that it did if we had not had the conflict resolution, mediation, and listening training that we had received. This is made evident by the fact that as our semester moved forward, our conflict resolution toolkit grew, and we became more comfortable with one another, the quality of our group work drastically increased. I think the small group approach is a very effective way of developing conflict resolution strategies, since it allows for a lot of direct dialogue, collaboration, and trust building between the members of said group. I was glad to work in a group and I really liked learning about this topic. I think this was the kind of ideal group project where I was truly able to learn more about the topic by being in a group than I would have if I did this entire thing independently."

Group work is a natural fit for conflict resolution courses. Students learn personal skills for dealing with conflict, and because they are learning these skills collaboratively, they are able to hold each other accountable for behavior that stereotypically corrupts group projects. Students also develop a deeper respect for the nature of relationships and interdependence in conflict. This process is a success because the lessons of managing personal conflict are at the core of the assignment and group process itself. Students read theory from experts in the field throughout the course, but in personally applying the theory and conflict resolution skills to their group project, they resolve not only the tension in their groups, but also the tension between theory and practice in the class as a whole. The final presentations show the real work in the class as bonded group members share a collective sigh of a job well done.

RECOMMENDED READINGS

Colbeck, Carol L., Susan E. Campbell, and Stefani A. Bjorklund. 2000. "Grouping in the Dark: What College Students Learn from Group Projects." *The Journal of Higher Education* 71 (1): 60–83.

Johnson, David W., Roger T. Johnson, and Karl A. Smith. 1998. "Cooperative Learning Returns to College: What Evidence is There that it Works?" *Change: The Magazine of Higher Learning* 30(4): 27–35.

Michaelsen, Larry K., L. Dee Fink, and Arletta Knight. 1997. "Designing Effective Group Activities: Lessons for Classroom Teaching and Faculty Development," in Deborah DeZure (ed.), *To Improve the Academy: Resources for Faculty, Instructional and Organizational Development*. Stillwater, OK: New Forums.

Oakley, Barbara, Richard M. Felder, Rebecca Brent, and Imad Elhajj. 2004. "Turning Student Groups into Effective Teams." *Journal of Student Centered Learning* 2 (1): 9–34.

United States Institute of Peace. 2017. "Conflict Styles Assessment." Available at <https://www.usip.org/public-education/students/conflict-styles-assessment>, last accessed June 23, 2017.

Wehr, Paul Ernest. 1979. *Conflict Regulation*. Boulder: Westview Press.

Withers, Bill and Keami D. Lewis. 2003. The Conflict and Communication Activity Book: 30 High-Impact Training Exercises for Adult Learners. New York: AMACOM.

Teaching Religion, Conflict, and Peace

TANYA B. SCHWARZ

Two dominant assumptions persist in both academic scholarship and broader public discourses vis-à-vis the role of religion in social and political life: religion contributes to division and discord, or, religion provides a unique and often-untapped resource for peace. Such assumptions rely on essentialist notions of what constitutes "religion," making discussions about religion, war, and peace particularly challenging in the university classroom. Given the often deep-seated assumptions that students carry about the role of religion in conflict and peace, as well as prevailing assumptions, in academic scholarship, about the inherent problems or benefits of religion, how should one go about teaching religion, conflict, and peace in the university classroom? One approach is to engage students in a kind of critical concept (de)formation early on in the course in order to unsettle students' assumptions about religion, more generally, as well as the role of religion in conflict and peacebuilding, in particular.

Does religion contribute to conflict? The narrative about the danger of religion is strong, especially in the context of global politics. Mythologies surrounding the Enlightenment and the Peace of Westphalia continue to promote the twin ideas that religion has been (largely) separated from global politics and that this is a good thing. Yet, after the end of the Cold War and increasingly after 9/11, scholars and others have suggested that religion is resurging in global politics and could, in fact, be a key factor in future international conflict. Those who suggest that religion will necessarily lead to conflict often rely on an essentialist view of religion. They treat religious values, for instance, as fixed entities within specific religious traditions, and suggest that those values are fundamentally incompatible across traditions.

Yet, while some view religion as inherently divisive and as a potential driver of conflict, others argue that religions offer unique and beneficial tools for peacebuilding. Some scholars and peacebuilding practitioners argue that religious organizations, in particular, are uniquely suited to peacebuilding projects because such organizations understand religious perspectives, they can draw on local religious institutions, and they approach peace from a holistic perspective—focusing on spiritual needs, as well as material. Similar to those who view religion as inherently problematic, these promoters of religion, often "essentialize" religion—treating religious traditions, communities, and values as fixed and monolithic. They might, for instance, emphasize certain interpretations of a religious text in a way that supports the notion that religions are inherently peaceful, while delegitimizing or simply neglecting other interpretations.

Given that assumptions about the inherent benefits or failings of religion are so prevalent in public discourse, teaching students about the role of religion in specific contexts of conflict or peacebuilding can be particularly problematic. Some students, for instance, assume that Islam is an inherently violent religion. Others assume that Christian development projects are hiding Christian organizations' "true" intent, which is to spread their faith. Other students view Buddhist monks as an unproblematic example of "religion doing good" in the world. These and similar assumptions gloss over complex historical, social, and political factors that shape how, why, and in what ways "religion" interacts with issues of conflict and peace.

Critical approaches to religion move beyond dichotomous frameworks of religion that treat religious traditions and communities as static and monolithic. These critical approaches draw on the works of Max Weber, Talal Asad, and others who have argued that religion is socially constructed, and thus malleable and dependent on a range of historical, social, and political factors. Not all scholars who study religion and global politics approach the subject from a critical perspective. Some simply treat religion as another factor that can be easily defined and measured. Yet critical approaches to religion, which tend to treat religion as lived and context-dependent, tend to do a better job of (1) accounting for the wide array of experiences, identities, and practices of so-called "religious" actors and (2) paying attention to the analytical and material relationship between religion and other political and social factors. Scholars like Mark Juergensmeyer, Mona Kanwal Sheikh, Cecelia Lynch, and others have provided important insights into, for instance, the motivations behind religious terrorism, how religion is securitized, and how faith-based aid organizations conceptualize their work within the context of the Global War on Terror—all while approaching religion as lived, socially constructed, and context dependent.

These and other critical scholars of religion continue to provide new ways to conceptualize and study this thing we call "religion." Lived approaches to religion, in particular, employed by Robert Orsi, Elizabeth Shakman Hurd, Erin Wilson, and others stress the ways that religion is lived, practiced, experienced, and embodied. Such approaches directly challenge the essentialization of religion by, in part, emphasizing the wide variances in how religion is conceptualized and experienced by religious actors themselves.

In the classroom, I draw on these critical approaches to religion—that employ a range of sociological and ethics-based techniques—encouraging students to look beyond hegemonic understandings that treat religion, or any particular religious tradition, as an "essentialized" and monolithic object. In order to engage with religion critically, however, most students must first directly engage, and perhaps even challenge, their own ingrained assumptions about religion. Students tend to think of religion as something that is relatively easy to define. In the classroom, I rely on a technique of critical concept (de)formation that directly challenges this assumption—providing the pedagogical space for students to grapple with the conceptual and ethical difficulties of formulating a universal definition of religion. In other words, in order to prepare students for the kind of critical analysis necessary for lived approaches to the study of religion, students must first directly engage with their assumptions about the topic. Thus, I begin all of my religion courses with an exercise that encourages students to deconstruct their conceptualizations of religion.

I often conduct this exercise on the first day of class before the students have completed any substantial readings for the course. I begin by asking the students to take 5–10 minutes to write down a definition of religion with an accompanying example of a specific religion. The writing component of the exercise is a low stakes assignment that enables students to take the time necessary to formulate their thoughts before engaging in discussion with others, which can be important when tackling intellectually complex issues like concept formation. We then discuss what the students have come up with. With each answer the students provide, however, I push back with a challenge to that answer. I provide three examples below of what this might look like and follow with a discussion of how these specific exercises are valuable for engaging, in the classroom, in a critical study of religion vis-à-vis peace and conflict.

Scenario 1: Some students view religion as a set of traditions or practices that are institutionalized in the form of churches, mosques, synagogues, and the like. Many of these students tend to conceptually distinguish spirituality and religion. While they view the two as related, in that each are connected to some sort of otherworldliness or transcendence, they see religion as a version that relies more on hierarchies and rules than spirituality. When a student offers this definition of religion, I counter by asking how often a person must attend a religious institution in order to identify as "religious" rather than "spiritual." This question leads to further discussions about who decides what label is appropriate. Should we, for instance, rely on a person's own understanding of how they understand themselves and their own relationship with religion or spirituality? Or can we make determinations of a person's religiosity based on specific empirical factors? Opening up this line of questioning unsettles the students' perceived objective analytical position—revealing alternative ways of knowing (and determining) what constitutes religion.

Scenario 2: When providing an example of what constitutes a religion, often students will refer to one or more of the "world religions" (e.g., Buddhism, Christianity, Hinduism, Islam, Judaism). When this occurs, I tell the students stories about several people I know who identify as non-practicing, non-believing Jews or Muslims. I then ask what implications these kinds of classifications might have for how one might categorize religion—especially religious identity. This line of questioning encourages students to think about how other identities related to culture and ethnicity might overlap with and/or might be more salient than religious identities in certain contexts and for certain actors.

Scenario 3: Some students inevitably refer to religion as a set of traditions or practices that promotes a particular ideological system-specific ideas about what constitutes a good life. In these discussions, I ask students whether, according to that definition, Marxism or capitalism also qualifies as a religion. By comparing definitions of religion to other value-based systems often not thought of as religious, I again encourage students to think more about the conceptual categories they use to define religion and to question whether or not those categories make any meaningful sense.

These three scenarios—which do not exhaust all of the questions and discussions I employ in this exercise, but are illustrative of the general approach—demonstrate how an educator might encourage students to deconstruct their ideas about religion. Encouraging students to reflexively engage with their own understandings about religion opens an intellectual space to think anew about what it means to talk about "religion" (and related categories like secularism) in global politics. Yet this does not mean leaving students with the idea that the concept of religion is meaningless. Nor do I provide students with an alternative definitive answer of what religion is or is not. Instead, my goal is to equip students with the critical tools necessary to analyze and problematize different understandings of, and approaches to, religion. As such, the rest of the course continues to grapple with the question of what constitutes religion, while also providing specific approaches for studying religion in ways that are attentive to social, political, and historical contexts, as well as relations of power.

Furthermore, while the aim of directly challenging students' understandings of religion is to open up an intellectual space for the critical analysis of religion in specific contexts of global politics, critically engaging with religion in contexts of peacebuilding and conflict, in particular, is especially important due to common assumptions about the role of religion in these areas. Challenging students to re-examine their own notions about what constitutes religion can also change the conversation about what role religion plays in specific contexts of conflict and peace.

The scenarios I laid out above provide good examples of how a critical concept (de)formation of religion can shed new light on the potential role of religion in peace and conflict. For instance, by unsettling the notion of objectivity in determining what is or is not religious, students begin to pay attention to how and why specific governmental actors might label a group like the Islamic State of Iraq and Syria (ISIS) as legitimately Islamic or not, and the potential consequences of that labeling on foreign policy and the actions of ISIS itself. By emphasizing how other kinds of identities (for example ethnic and cultural) can overlap with religious ones, students begin to question whether religious identity differences are necessarily divisive, and if not, whether interfaith dialogue is, perhaps, in some contexts, more prone to create, rather than mitigate, difference. And, by revealing the similarities between "secular" and "religious" ideological systems, students broaden their analytical lenses to think about what other factors, besides religion, might be contributing to conflict (or peace). Thus, encouraging students to reflexively engage with their own assumptions about religion can also lead to a broader reassessment about the key factors shaping peace and conflict.

In public discourse religion is often framed as something that is inherently problematic—leading to divisions, and eventually conflict—or as an untapped resource for peace. As a result, a critical engagement with questions about religion's relationship with conflict and peace in the university classroom often requires a direct engagement with students' underlying assumptions about religion that feed into broader notions about these issues. A rich body of interdisciplinary work has emerged that moves beyond essentialist frameworks of religion, and instead, treats religion as socially constructed, lived, and context-dependent. Such works challenge popular assertions about the inherent dangers or benefits of religion in social and political life. Before delving into these arguments, however, students can benefit from a direct engagement with their own deep-seated assumptions about religion. The goal of the exercise I outlined here is not to indoctrinate students in a particular definition of religion, or to suggest that religion is or is not inherently peaceful or dangerous, but to, instead, provide students with the intellectual tools for a critical exploration of religion, conflict, and peace in the university classroom.

RECOMMENDED READINGS

Asad, Talal. 1993. *Genealogies of Religion: Discipline and Reasons of Power in Christianity and Islam.* Baltimore: The Johns Hopkins University Press.

Asad, Talal. 2003. *Formations of the Secular: Christianity, Islam, Modernity.* Stanford: Stanford University Press.

Juergensmeyer, Mark. 2001. *Terror in the Mind of God: The Global Rise of Religious Violence*. Berkeley: University of California Press.

Juergensmeyer, Mark. 2008. *Global Rebellion: Religious Challenges to the Secular State from Christian Militias to Al Qaeda*. Berkeley: University of California Press.

Kanwal Sheikh, Mona. 2014. "The Religious Challenge to Securitization Theory." *Millennium: Journal of International Studies* 43 (1):252–272. doi:10.1177/0305829814540853.

Lynch, Cecelia. 2009. "A Neo-Weberian Approach to Religion in International Politics." *International Theory* 1 (3):381–408. doi:10.1017/S1752971909000116.

Lynch, Cecelia. 2014. "A Neo-Weberian Approach to Studying Religion and Violence." *Millennium: Journal of International Studies* 41 (3):273–298.

Omer, Atalia, R. Scott Appleby, and David Little (eds). 2015. *The Oxford Handbook of Religion, Conflict, and Peacebuilding*. New York: Oxford University Press.

Orsi, Robert A. 2010. *The Madonna of 115th Street: Faith and Community in Italian Harlem, 1880–1950, Third Edition*. New Haven, CT: Yale University Press.

Schwarz, Tanya B. 2018. *Faith-Based Organizations in Transnational Peacebuilding*. Lanham, MD: Rowman & Littlefield International.

Shakman Hurd, Elizabeth. 2008. *The Politics of Secularism in International Relations*. Princeton, NJ: Princeton University Press.

Shakman Hurd, Elizabeth. 2015. *Beyond Religious Freedom: The New Global Politics of Religion*. Princeton, NJ: Princeton University Press.

Weber, Max. 1993. *The Sociology of Religion, Fourth Edition*. Translated by Ephraim Fischoff. Boston: Beacon Press.

Wilson, Erin K. 2012. *After Secularism: Rethinking Religion in Global Politics*. New York: Palgrave Macmillan.

Idealism Versus Pragmatism in Teaching Peace in Pakistan

ZAHID SHAHAB AHMED

At the start of the "War on Terror" in 2001, Pakistan's education systems came under the international spotlight. Particular attention was paid to the quality of curricula and teaching styles in madrassas (Islamic seminaries) and public schools. Initially, focus and implementation of peace education programs were limited to madrassas, for example, through early initiatives of the Washington-based International Center for Religion and Diplomacy in 2004. While "teaching peace" programs have been going on now for over a decade, little is known about their impact and the realities in which they operate. Peace education in Pakistan demonstrates a perfect case to understand the struggle of implementing organizations to maintain a balance between idealism and pragmatism. The context in which the education of wars is in the mainstream, for example, through the glorification of wars and war heroes in public school textbooks, teaching peace is merely limited to the realm of nongovernmental organizations (NGOs), mainly funded by Western donors. The limited scope of teaching peace programs is further constrained by the limited capacity of peace education, implementation on an ad hoc basis, irrelevant contents, the shortage of quality teachers, domination of Western values, the absence of NGOs' network, and the hostility of the government and extremist groups.

Western approaches of peace and conflict are dominantly applied in teaching peace programs in Pakistan. The exported models largely focus on the implementation/development/teaching of individual skills, such as interpersonal conflict management, mediation, and conflict resolution. Pakistan, however, requires a collective approach rather than an individualistic Western approach. Another issue in teaching peace programs is the placement of teaching about wars in connection to peacemaking. None of the peace education programs examined by the author included topics relevant to wars, such as, for instance, economic and human costs of wars. An overwhelming majority of teachers interviewed by the author stressed the need of curriculum reforms to ensure sustainability of teaching peace. Idealistic thinking, however, dominates the design and application of many of the peace education programs.

Unfortunately, idealistic thinking prevails in the design and application of projects for teaching peace. The Community World Service has produced several books in Urdu to teach peace but it has not made any effort to promote those books for inclusion in mainstream education. Similar is the case of books produced by the United Nations Children's Fund. The disconnect between efforts at the grassroots level and policymaking level is based on a range of factors, such as the limited financial and human resources, and the opposition from Islamists to educational reforms.

Most of the short-term projects lack proper research, and this leads to many teaching peace projects having little or no relevance to the target communities. A major hurdle is to counter the influence of school textbooks promoting stereotyping and intolerance. There is, however, no NGO that addresses this aspect. From Kursheed Kamal Aziz's *Murder of History* to Zahid Shahab Ahmed and Michelle Baxter's *Attitudes of Teachers in India and Pakistan: Texts and Contexts,* there is evidence of textbooks in Pakistan containing factual errors, bias, and hate toward a number of non-Muslims and nations. It is thus vital for the ongoing teaching peace programs to deliver knowledge and alternatives in order to build resilience among children to counter extremist ideologies that have now gone beyond the school textbooks to social media. Another challenge is to ensure that students retain the knowledge acquired from such programs and apply this knowledge to their lives. This can only happen if such initiatives are long term and involve parents and community members. Unfortunately, a lot of teaching peace projects are designed to have minimal or no impact from the beginning; for instance, at the stage of project conceptualization when the program staff of an NGO grapples with the puzzle of idealism versus pragmatism.

While there is no harm in aiming for an ideal society that is free from violence of any kind, there is a need to be realistic and practical. Here the focus is again on the application of the knowledge that students gain through peace education programs. The Charter for Compassion works in mainly private sector schools in Karachi, the biggest city of Pakistan, to teach compassionate skills as per the philosophy of Karen Armstrong. Despite being a very innovative and creative program, which is implemented by a young passionate team of trainers, the project does not engage the participants in discussion on the following questions: Are there times when showing compassion can get you into danger? How can students apply their compassionate skills, such as courage, if a place is attacked by a suicide bomber? Without answering questions such as these, the program runs the risk of being ineffective in offering needed skills to the students. This issue raises more questions: Are we giving students what they need? Do we do need assessment in classrooms before and during our training programs? Do we identify future peace leaders and stay engaged with them? Unfortunately, the answer to such questions is "no." This is mainly because the majority of peace education projects in Pakistan are donor-driven, meaning not designed based on a long-term engagement with either a theme or a target community.

Rising violent religious extremism and widespread insecurity are main concerns for the local NGOs and their international partners working on preventing violent extremism through education. For example, there are numerous examples of NGO offices and workers being attacked by terrorists. Threats of rampant religious extremism and terrorism compel the NGOs and their international partners to apply conflict-sensitive approaches to their projects. This pragmatic approach limits the scope of development projects in general and peace education in particular as, for example, this approach restricts the programs to areas that are relatively peaceful. There is another major limitation of teaching peace programs failing to target relevant groups, such as the ones under direct risk of extremist ideologies.

Beyond approaching relevant communities is the need to address pertinent issues at hand. An examination of the program run by Jamia Naeemia, a *madrassa* based in Lahore, demonstrated a visible pragmatic approach in which the institute's administration decided to avoid the addition of a sectarian (Shi'ite versus Sunni) fissure in the subjects covered during the training. Here it is important to underline the fact that *madrassas* are divided based on sectarian lines, therefore, a Sunni *madrassa* cannot easily talk about the sectarian divide without facing a conflict with Shi'ite *madrassas*. Jamia Naeemia or its current leadership is extra cautious because the institute's founding father, Mufti Sarfraz Ahmed Naeemi, was killed inside the *madrassa* by the Tehrik-i-Taliban terrorists in 2009. Thus, threats to personal life are real for groups countering violent extremism in Pakistan.

The limited scope of teaching peace programs is reflected in their contents. NGOs find it problematic to work with *madrassas* that openly declare peace education a Western project by considering issues, such as tolerance, religious harmony, and human rights, as Western values. Due to these limitations, peace education programs have reached a minor fraction of the country's 35,000 *madrassas*. Pragmatism has compelled NGOs to approach *madrassas* as per convenience. Many teaching peace programs have been implemented in urban area *madrassas* that are easy to work with in terms of accessibility and communication. NGOs have not approached *madrassas* where traditional clerics tend to criticize modern technologies such as, for instance, the Internet, as a Western instrument responsible for weakening Muslim cultures and values.

As it happens, thousands of *madrassas* do not teach modern science and technology. Considering limited funding for peace, NGOs should focus on institutions, communities, and groups that do not just need an intervention, but where they could introduce desired social/behavioral changes more effectively to build resilience against violent extremism. Without focusing on this aspect, many of the examined programs in Pakistan have been converting the converted due to the lack of relevance to the local settings

In addition to *madrassas* avoiding the sectarian divide in Pakistan, peace education programs across the board have not moved beyond issues such as interfaith harmony, a basic understanding of conflict resolution, human rights and peace, and the concept of peace in Islam. None of the examined projects focused on disarmament, environmental security, and structural violence. This cannot be labeled as being pragmatic because various NGOs lack the capacity to produce, based on solid research, relevant peace education contents. Due to the availability of foreign aid, several NGOs claim to have expertise in peace education, but in reality, they lack the capacity to do full justice to the teaching of peace. Without mentioning the name of the organization for ethical considerations, the author would like to share an interesting case when an NGO claiming to have substantial experience in peace education decided to outsource the development of teaching peace material to a third party. It is no surprise that the outcome was a disaster.

On the other hand, besides working to avoid contentious issues, NGOs have also been practical and creative in their selection of project titles. Unfortunately, the word "peace" carries negative connotations in Pakistan. There is a widespread perception that such programs are based on Western propaganda against Islam and Pakistan. To counter this perception, many NGOs have developed peace education material based on Islamic teachings. The prominent examples are of the books produced on Islam and conflict resolution/peace by the United States Institute of Peace and the Peace and Education Foundation. An important aspect of the methodology behind the mentioned books was the involvement and endorsement of prominent Muslim scholars from Pakistan. This strategy has worked for many groups who continue to work with a range of actors, especially *madrassas* teachers. Prominent examples are that of Jamia Naeemi and the Peace and Education Development (PEAD) Foundation, which have developed peace education programs with the key principle that peace and conflict resolution should be presented as inherently Islamic values. This has definitely helped the organizations working this way to develop a good rapport with the local communities. Another issue is that NGOs have been hesitant to use the word "peace" in the titles of their programs. For example, a teaching peace project of PEAD Foundation is entitled "Strengthening Social Cohesion and Resilience through Education Initiative." This particular concern about negative perceptions of "peace" is more prevalent in *madrassas*.

The success of any educational project rests on the quality of its teachers. As explored in the author's research, most of the teaching peace programs lacked quality teachers. The teachers of many programs were not trained and therefore were incapable of imparting key skills like critical thinking, particularly to students in *madrassas* and public schools. In addition, teachers' training programs had limited success because of a limited capacity of trainers and the short-term nature of interventions. Considering teachers in *madrassas* and public schools are not well educated and trained, there is a need for long-term interventions to introduce teachers to theories and practices relevant to teaching in general and teaching peace in particular.

B earing in mind the sensitivities linked with working in Pakistan, non-state actors have to be extra cautious. There is an unwritten agreement between donors and local organizations to refrain from publicizing the names of donors, often from Western countries, in their project material. Considering the presence of violent religious extremism and anti-Western sentiments, this is a pragmatic approach. Organizations in conflict-affected areas, particularly in Khyber Pakhtunkhwa, did not advertise that their work was funded by foreign organizations because that revelation could have had severe security repercussions. In the region of Swat, which was under the control of the Taliban during 2007–09, Swat Youth Front did not disclose the name of its London-based donor. This also means that members of the donors also did not visit the project site, which on one hand raises concerns about monitoring and evaluations, but on the other hand, it was also not feasible due to security reasons. It is important to highlight that often the visits of Western staff to project areas in rural Pakistan have created difficulties for local NGOs. NGOs with larger canvas, however, could share the information about their well-established or reputable donors from, for example, the United Nations, and the European Union.

In practice, peace education is heavily dependent on pedagogies to promote critical thinking and the transfer of knowledge to equip students with conflict resolution skills. In the context of Pakistan, peace education is needed to provide students and teachers with knowledge and thinking to counter extremist ideologies. Here it is important to talk about the work of Swat Youth Front, which is based in the region that was once under the control of local Taliban. Through the organization's program, students were encouraged to write on issues of human rights, women's rights in Islam, post-conflict reconstruction, and contemporary sociopolitical issues in a magazine called *Naveed-e-Sahar*. This initiative helped develop students' knowledge on critical issues and writing as well as on information-sharing skills.

Excluding the cases in which peace education has been localized as per the realities of Pakistan, there are examples of initiatives being inspired by global approaches on the subject. The Grammar School Rawalpindi is a private school that has modeled its peace education curricula on the United Nations Educational, Scientific and Cultural Organization's guidelines. Teachers of the school have been discussing the progressive phase of Muslims, including times when Muslims were scientifically advanced. A teacher from the school shared that it is difficult to teach peace when the realities outside the classroom do not match up with the topics studied as this counters peace education taught on an ad hoc basis for about an hour every week. The teachers also said that the new media, especially social media, exposes students to negative ideologies that the school's limited teaching peace model does not address.

Among the successful cases is the initiative of Paiman Alumni Trust, (henceforth Paiman). The organization runs peace education projects in Peshawar to train teachers and students at two local private schools through an integrated approach. In this model, teaching peace is included in regular primary- and secondary-level curriculum. Students were interviewed from a participating school and they reflected a clear understanding of the concepts of peace and conflict by linking key features of learning to the notions of justice, development, and security.

This level of understanding of peace and security was not observed in students of other projects that were implemented on an ad hoc basis, meaning not integrated into regular education like the case of Paiman's project. Paiman has an idealistic approach to present this project as a model for mainstream peace education in other schools, but it is unlikely to happen unless the government authorities are convinced to mainstream peace education contents and pedagogies as part of a long-term measure to prevent/counter violent extremism through education in Pakistan. That would require inclusion of peace education contents in textbooks and trainings for teachers in teacher training centers.

Despite the remarkable growth of the peacebuilding sector in Pakistan since 2001, there is the absence of a forum and/or a network that could bring various groups teaching peace together. This is due to several reasons, such as the competition among NGOs for funding. The lack of networking among NGOs poses a serious threat to their own survival when there is an ongoing governmental crackdown on the NGOs. Also, this leads to wasting energy and resources due to the absence of mechanisms through which knowledge and expertise could be shared instead of everyone reinventing the wheel in the form of replicating peace education material. Working jointly will help in strengthening advocacy for the inclusion of peace education in the public education system.

Unlike the mainstream education of wars, the field of peace education is under-developed in Pakistan. The case of NGOs teaching peace in Pakistan is a mixed bag of successes and failures, and demonstrates their struggle to maintain a balance between idealism and pragmatism. While some aim for the stars in terms of teaching for an ideal peaceful society, others miss the mark by teaching irrelevant contents. Many NGOs studied by the author lacked the capacity to produce contextually relevant contents. This limitation was reflected in the poor implementation of several programs.

The organizations teaching peace navigate in a highly sensitive territory in which a slight mistake can lead to disastrous consequences (e.g., through direct attacks of violent extremist groups). This phenomenon is aggravated by the government's protection of extremist groups and the crackdown on NGOs. Thus, local NGOs work very carefully and avoid the risk of working where they should ideally work and with contents that they should ideally promote. Despite all these challenges, teaching peace is important to prevent/counter violent extremist ideologies in Pakistan. One of the constraints of teaching peace in Pakistan is the three-tier system of education in which each system—*madrassas*, public schools, and private schools—has limited or no interaction with the other. This ultimately demands customized programs to address the needs of each system.

ACKNOWLEDGMENTS

This article is based on the author's extensive research of NGOs teaching peace across Pakistan. The author has written permissions from the mentioned organizations to cite their work.

RECOMMENDED READINGS

Ahmed, Zahid Shahab, and Michelle A. Baxter. 2007. *Attitudes of Teachers in India and Pakistan: Texts and Contexts.* New Delhi: WISCOMP.

Ahmed, Zahid Shahab. 2017. *Peace Education in Pakistan*. Washington, DC: United States Institute of Peace. Accessed October 10, 2017. https://www.usip.org/publications/2017/03/peace-education-pakistan.

Armstrong, Karen. 2011. *Twelve Steps to a Compassionate Life*. London: The Bodley Head.

Aziz, Khursheed Kamal. 1993. *Murder of History: A Critique of History Textbooks Used in Pakistan*. Lahore: Sang-e-Meel Publications.

Durrani, Naureen, and Máiréad Dunne. 2010. "Curriculum and National Identity: Exploring the Links between Religion and Nation in Pakistan." *Journal of Curriculum Studies* 42 (2):215–40.

Gienger, Viola. 2017. "Pakistani Educator Takes Risks to Promote Culture of Peace in Schools. Charter for Compassion." Accessed September 20, 2017. https://charterforcompassion.org/pakistani-educator-takes-risks-to-promote-culture-of-peace-in-schools.

Grare, Frédéric. 2007. "The Evolution of Sectarian Conflicts in Pakistan and the Ever-Changing Face of Islamic Violence." *South Asia: Journal of South Asian Studies* 30 (1):127–43.

Hoti, Amineh, and Zahid Shahab Ahmed. 2016. "Peace Education in Pakistan: A Case Study of the Centre for Dialogue and Action, FC College University, Pakistan," In *Handbook of Research on Promoting Global Peace and Civic Engagement through Education*, edited by Kshama Pandey, Pratibha Upadhyay and Amit Jaiswal, 323–37. Hershey, PA: IGI Global.

Peace Direct 2017. Local Approaches to Preventing Violent Extremism in Pakistan. Accessed October 7, 2017. https://www.peacedirect.org/publications/local-approaches-preventing-violent-extremism-pakistan/.

Rupert, James. 2015. *Teaching Peace in Pakistan's Turbulent Mega-City: A Campaign in Karachi Reaches Children via School, Art, Sports*. Washington, DC: United States Institute of Peace. Accessed October 1, 2017. https://www.usip.org/publications/2015/11/teaching-peace-pakistans-turbulent-mega-city.

Sajjad, Fatima, Daniel J. Christie, and Laura K. Taylor. 2017. "De-Radicalizing Pakistani Society: The Receptivity of Youth to a Liberal Religious Worldview." *Journal of Peace Education* 14 (2):195–214.

Sheikh, Rameez Ahmed. 2016. "Review of Peace Education in Pakistan." Accessed September 22, 2017. http://www.peace-ed-campaign.org/wp-content/uploads/2016/03/Paper-of-Peace-Education-by-Rameez-Ahmed-Sheikh.pdf.

Smith, Alan. 2010. *The Influence of Education on Conflict and Peace Building*. Paris: UNESCO. Accessed October 5, 2017. http://unesdoc.unesco.org/images/0019/001913/191341e.pdf.

The Intrigue of Peace and War Curriculum in Africa

KUDAKWASHE CHIRAMBWI

The stigmatization and differentiation of students on one hand, and the crystallization and solidification of teachers' political ideologies on the other, are acute in peace education and war curriculum in Africa. Yet the regular school curriculum on peace education is increasingly accentuated as an answer to achieving peace, security, and development—this at a time when African countries are aflame with civil wars, ethnic divide, resource-instigated conflicts, and terrorism, all culminating into grossly horrifying human rights abuses. Barely do we see peace curriculum as a paradox, with competing roles of supporting violence on one hand and peace on the other.

Incrementally, the United Nations Educational, Scientific and Cultural Organization (UNESCO) and the African Union have prioritized education for peace as a fundamental right in learning institutions in Africa. A more recent example is the candid statement by the UNESCO Director-General, Irina Bokova, during the United Nations General Assembly's 72nd high level session on "Making Education for Peace" held on September 20, 2017. She remarked, "We need to teach peace to prevent terrorism from teaching our children. Educational institutions must teach the concept of peace and non-violence as an 'alternative option' to resolve conflicts." Bokova claimed then that education is the "soft-power for peace." Even the United Nations Security Council Resolution 2250 places trust on making education for peace as an alternative antidote to violent extremism and radicalism. Similarly, Sustainable Development Goal 4 considers education as having a trickle-down effect to sustainable peace Goal 16. Despite the phenomenal policy focus and growth in peace education, the conversation that is not taking place, but that needs to happen, is on how the curriculum and its purveyors, the teachers, are reproducing and sustaining violence and intolerance.

What is clear here is the abuse of peace education curriculum to Islamify schools that further perpetuate belligerents rather than intended peace. It has equally escaped scholars and policy makers' attention to examine how, masked as peace education, uniformed soldiers, disguised as teaching practical life skills on civic defense, use schools and universities for purposes of militarizing the youth. The thrust and intent of this essay is to reveal how regular school curriculum, if overlooked, prepares for war and violence in the name of peace.

What is the compelling need for peace education in Africa? Generally, the current youth bulge is the largest in the history of Africa amounting to 226 million (19 percent) of the 1.2 billion global population of youth. United Nations has estimated that youth in Africa would have increased by 42 percent by 2030. The figure is expected to triple by 2055. The demographic imperative places the centrality of peace education curriculum that capacitates youth with requisite skills to oppose all forms of violence. Faced with ten active conflicts in Africa, the African Union dubbed 2017 as the Year of the Youth, and United Nations hosted the 2017 International Youth Day with the theme "Youth Building Peace," which is an acknowledgment of youth's potential to oppose violence.

Three arguments are usually peddled to justify youth's involvement in peace education. First, for a decade now, a large body of evidence has accumulated showing young people as catalysts for change. This, however, is counter-argued by the truism that "war has been invented to give young men something to do so they don't undermine the order of things." Incidentally, concerns are raised that about 40 percent of the global number of child soldiers are located on the African continent. Second, there is rich literature that conceptualizes youth as having a massive influence in several spheres of life. Yet they are often seen as a potential destabilizing factor. Third, youth are creative, innovative, and possess imaginative energy that is a critical ingredient necessary in preventing violence and war.

These attributes alone, however, are insufficient to bring peace to a context of increasing structural violence and an entrenched neo-patrimonial governance system. For instance, although the course content is calibrated to prepare students to understand the complexity of the world and to retool them with values and skills necessary to engineer change and progressive thinking, does it meet their needs around day-to-day violence? Consider the long-term impact of their activities as encapsulated in the Campaign Statement of the Global Campaign for Peace: "A culture of peace will be achieved when citizens of the world understand global problems; have the skills to resolve conflict constructively; know and live by international standards of human rights, gender and racial equality;

appreciate cultural diversity; and respect the integrity of the Earth. Such learning cannot be achieved without intentional, sustained and systematic education for peace."

Yet hardly do we ask ourselves the practical relevance of peace education curriculum in contexts of learning taking place in communities disrupted by conflict; neo-patrimonialism; frustrations from enormously complex demographic changes in the "youth bulge"; debilitating political economies with their attendant problems of low educational attainment, unemployment, and poverty; low levels of educational attainment; and high levels of gun violence, strongmen, and high-powered wealthy businessmen. What continues to evade scholarly attention, however, is to examine the best ways teachers can cultivate a new style of critical thinking and imbue students with capacities to formulate better questions and answers to concerns in our daily lives when there are limits to what is available for the youth.

Although peace curricula are designed for a wide range of students, from primary and secondary levels, to undergraduate and postgraduate students, significant challenges remain: First is the trauma from the horror of violence. The body of students now being taught peace have either experienced the horror of civil wars or have suffered physical violence as in the case of Rwanda, South Sudan, the Democratic Republic of the Congo, Mali, and Chad. Reliving conflict and flight and fear and terror constricts potential for critical thinking, thereby creating space in the "archaeology of mind" for apprehensiveness, tension, distrust, and nervousness. Second, of the 263 million children and youth who are out of school worldwide, Sub-Saharan Africa has 60 percent of school dropouts. These dropouts suffer from stigmatization and differentiation, which compels them to compensate through an unofficial education system.

Third, several interconnecting and often competing dimensions of peace and war education take place at three distinct levels of learning in Africa: formal, nonformal, and informal. Formal pedagogy is where peace education and war are taught in a structured, systematic, and organized curriculum with clearly defined clerical-administrative procedures. It is, however, rendered more proscriptive and manipulative than heuristic. Nonformal is often called open-learning, as acquisition of knowledge takes place outside the classroom setting. For instance, students interact with uniformed soldiers, militants, or peacekeepers such as U.S. Special Command Army Green Berets in Niger and Mali. Informal or unofficial learning occurs when students acquire knowledge from incidences of violent conflicts.

Despite overlaps among these domains, competition exists where informal learning often dwarfs the formal. This obviously does not provide opportunities for peacebuilding. As reinforced by Thomas Ward et al., "the legitimacy of schools is based upon their role as 'credentialising' agencies while non-formal education will derive its legitimacy only from its ability to meet real social needs." Fourth, most peace curricula in Africa are introduced after the violent conflicts, and therefore appear more as reactionary public emergency courses than preventive and long term. Illustrative is the Democratic Republic of Congo (DRC), which introduced a Civics and Moral peace education course in 2007 in response to violent crimes. In the same year, 2007, Kenya mounted a generic schools-wide peace course in response to violent elections instigated by inter-ethnic tensions. Similarly, Côte d'Ivoire, in response to the impact of post-election crisis (2010–2011) introduced a Citizenship and Human Rights Course in 2012 in school curricula. More concerting is how the courses are taught along ethnic identities and divisions, which further reinforces and celebrates differential identities that initially caused the resultant conflict.

T he most disconcerting issue, however, in formal classroom-based peace education is the monopoly of knowledge sustained by a cosmopolitan group of peace education "experts" in Africa. Four groups of peace education experts have emerged: first are the inside–insiders. These are African peace educators schooled in countries of origin whose curricula are informed by culture, history, and conflict experiences. The problem is, they are trapped in the error of thinking beyond culture and history. Second: the inside–outsiders. These are indigenous peace and war educators with Western constructs. Viewed as subject expert academics, they are trusted to possess unique knowledge acquired through graduate schools and career experience from overseas peacebuilding research institutes and think tanks. These teachers who acquired their degrees outside Africa rely heavily on the application of liberal ready-made theoretical frameworks underpinning peace discourse that ignore localized conceptual vocabularies that advance self-understanding for Africans. Their peace curricula focus primarily on stabilizing a failed/weak/stressed Africa, terrorism, war, and poverty. Third: the outsiders–insiders. These are composed of Western expatriate peace educators who claim to see Africa through the eyes of Africans. Their curricula are of securitization of terrorism, ungoverned spaces, development, and poverty. Last are the outside–outsiders. These are overseas interpretivists who have never spent time with the Africans they are writing about, but use a complex discourse of liberal peace and securitization of development. Most teachers, however, from the inside–insiders category tend to adopt ideologies from the inside–outsiders in a bid to achieve legitimacy from the outside–outsiders, who are the legitimacy granters and often fund peace education programs in Africa. Herein lies a clear clash of civilizations in African peace education curricula.

Critics of peace curricula dismiss African peace education as a Western creation, as a grammar of governmentality, and clearly as an ideological plot to perpetuate securitization and control of Africa. Addressing peace educators on the need to introduce peace and conflict resolution in the education curriculum in Zambia, the government representative, Mr. Mbulakulima, lobbied for the promotion of Ubuntu peace education, an African philosophy that places emphasis on our common humanity and provides guidance on how human beings should relate with the universe. He emphasized, "Let us reorient our society on the need to observe good morals, with the spirit of Ubuntu." Barely do we read of peace education curriculum informed by the Ubuntu theoretical framework. Whose peace and what peace are students learning given that the curriculum suffers from what Desai calls "expert ignorance?"

We tend to overlook the complexities around complicity of teachers as purveyors of violence through peace education curriculum. First, the teachers have a monopoly to choose the contents and pedagogy of the curriculum. Second, some of the teachers belong to the war-veteran fraternity who participated in the factional liberation struggle. More often than not, they are greatly influenced by war-time ideology, partisanship, and "ethicist ideology." As such, the teachers who have instigated inter-ethnic clashes in Kenya and Rwanda are potentially biased in implementing a neutral peace and war curricula. Because of the contentious ethnic divide, teachers, as reflected in post-genocide peace curriculum in Rwanda, continue to crystallize their identities, stigmatize those in opposition—something we ignore to investigate—how peace solidifies differential identities among students.

The teachers carry deep psychological scars from memories of war and are therefore potentially less neutral in implementing peace curricula. Illustrative is a case from Côte d'Ivoire where, out of 984 secondary school teachers surveyed on causes of crisis, the research unearthed a sharp division based on ethnoreligious lines between those who supported the former President Laurent Gbagbo and the incumbent Ivorian President Alassane Ouattara. They differed strongly about the causes and the main culprits of the crisis. As such the content of peace education reflects positionality, biases, crystallization, and solidification of political affiliation.

The ex-combatants-cum-teachers' personal but dominant views often strongly collide with liberal peace curriculum of achieving peace by peaceful means. This continues to violate the core values of an effective peace educator, namely independence, neutrality, and impartiality, reflexivity, and objectivity. All too familiar topics in peace and war education oscillate between nationalistic and factionalist discourses, with examples and case studies that are crisis-oriented rather than early warning designs that predict conflict. As in the case of Burkina Faso, Cape Verde, Cote d'Ivoire, The Gambia, Ghana, Kenya, Lesotho, Liberia, Nigeria, Zambia Zimbabwe, and South Africa, patriotism, reactionism, and militarism are components of taught courses.

The teacher and reading literature continue to make peace a hostage to war and violence. Education for peace in Africa gives us an invaluable perspective of how, inadvertently, it has become education for war, where curriculum and books tend to militarize students and society. For example, the Government of Zimbabwe blocked war veteran Agrippa Mutambara's book, *The Rebel in Me,* from being taught in secondary schools where students are expected to learn history of the liberation struggle. The author was a ZANLA Guerrilla Commander in the Rhodesian Bush War, 1974–1980. In Côte d'Ivoire, on the other hand, the book, *Why I Became a Rebel,* written by Guillaume Soro, the current President of the National Assembly, is used as a reference book by some factional teachers.

S uch literature presents war as the only possibility to resolve future conflicts as it celebrates intolerance, win/lose, confrontation, and male dominance over nonviolence and negotiated dispute resolution. From such books students learn of war as a means of pursuing peace. Violence is depicted as a tool for freedom, peace, and development, and that military action is deployed to justify change, ignoring alternative possibilities of pursuing the same change by peaceful means. As well, lessons learned from the 2011 Tunisian Revolution and Arab Spring counterargue that violence does bring freedom and democracy. To date, however, the traces of the Revolution have been more violence, unprecedented levels of unemployment and economic stagnation, and an increased number of extremist militia groups.

Education is a powerful tool that can be wielded to create a war mentality, rather than critical thinking required for peacebuilding. In most African countries, the army comes to schools, under the cover of peace education, to conduct lectures, exhibitions, and defense techniques on how students should protect themselves in cases of attack. Certainly soldiers have neither pedagogical skills nor experience to offer lessons in schools. More importantly, students are made to touch the gun as a form of inducting them into military life. Clearly, most schools in DRC, Mali, and Central African Republic involve students in military service without evaluating the educative effects of regular interaction with armed soldiers/ militias and handling guns.

This observation leads to my next argument that peace and war institutions in Africa continue to prop up militarized civilian-based defense systems, with school-going youth becoming the majority of vigilantes and brigades as in the case of Mali, DRC, Chad, and Nigeria. In South Sudan, DRC, and Niger uniformed soldiers and militants use schools as barracks, influencing students to see the military as an attractive career. In countries such as Kenya and Somalia, students are conjoined to the Ministries of Defence where they collaborate with the army and other security agencies to defend the state. Here, through peace education curriculum, students are saddled with the responsibility to protect the state.

A question remains, however. How can formal and informal peace education curriculum assist in transforming from a culture of war to a culture of peace and from a culture of law of force (soldiers in schools) to force of law? For example, in response to schoolgirls kidnapped from a school in Chibok, the Nigerian Defence Ministry militarized schools by building ditches around schools as buffers to stop Boko Haram fighters from abducting students and teachers. In Mogadishu, Somalia, armed soldiers have been planted around exam sites to prevent Al-Shabaab militants from attacking high school students who sat down to write their final exams for the first time in decades. Can military strategies be the best alternatives to make education safe? Martin Luther King Jr. consistently agitated for a social change that comes through nonviolent action, where peace values "will lay hands on the world order and say of war, 'This way of settling differences is not just.'" Further, King warned of war as "the chain of reaction of evil," as well as, "wars producing more wars must be broken, or we shall be plunged into the dark abyss of annihilation."

The claim that education is the best investment for the future of peace and resilience of societies in tension may not lend credence to the Nigerian case study and in Africa more generally. For instance, there is remarkable effort by the Government of Plateau in Nigeria to use peace education in primary and secondary schools to tackle radicalism of youth by Boko Haram. Extremism has become a part of the regular school curriculum on peace. The language of hate and intolerance is deployed, mislabeling Boko Haram militants as terrorists.

The extent that the curriculum addresses de-radicalization is not yet clear. What is clear, however, is the abuse of peace education curriculum by the ruling and governing elites to Islamify schools that, if continued unreformed, will perpetuate belligerents rather than the intended peace. The regular school curriculum that prepares for war in the name of peace addresses the Islamic movement as radical and dangerous, and therefore worth eliminating, something that solidifies an "in-group versus out-group" and "us versus them" mentality. For example, countries with large Muslim populations are misconstrued as dangerous. The largely Christian-dominated Southern Africa countries are perceived less hostile than Central, West, East, and Horn of Africa. Horn of Africa and East Africa for instance, are distorted as an "arch of instability," with countries such as Somalia, Djibouti Kenya, Zanzibar, and Tanzania heavily securitized. The peace education curricula presented in this "arch of instability" reinforce and solidify discrimination, stigmatization, and categorization of competing ethnic groups, which is sufficient fodder for future violence.

The discourse on "war on terror" has seen ruling elites benefiting from resources and military assistance from the West. As observed by Claire Metelits, "if leaders are faced with domestic unrest, they need only cry 'terrorist' to attract resources to subdue challengers." Peace education has been used as a cover by ruling and governing elite for political expedience, yet they ignore addressing the root causes of insurgence, and why groups such as Yan Tatsine in Nigeria feel betrayed by Muslim teachers and Western education. Western education was promoted among the Southerners, side-lining the largely Islamic Northerners. Education to the Southerners meant upward mobility, easy access to political power, better-paying jobs, and better services.

Similarly in Rwanda, rarely do we recognize the role of skewed curriculum played in significantly contributing to the 100 days massacre—the genocide. The colonial master, Belgium's "divide and rule" saw education being distributed along ethnic identities and divisions in which the minority Tutsi had more access and upward mobility than the majority Hutu who were highly restricted. Ethnic hierarchy was taught at the formative years of children. In classrooms, it was a rule for students to verbally identify themselves as either Hutu or Tutsi or carry ethnic identity cards, which inadvertently resulted in discrimination, perpetuation of ethnic superiority, and resistance. Such inequalities led to a 100-day-long bloodbath.

What can peace teachers do to, first, reform curriculum to ensure peace education is not abused by ruling and governing elites, and second, ensure the current curriculum does not redraw the ethnic boundaries that reproduces tension among students and society? Clearly, in Africa, if peace education curricula remain unreformed they have that propensity to create a circle of violence. In the case of Rwanda 1.2 million children were left orphaned, 100,000 living in child-headed households and 100,000 internally and externally displaced. The post-genocide peace education curriculum has to be continuously re-written to address inter-ethnic cooperation in a current context where traumatized teachers, students, and literature are still differentiated on ethnic lines.

Education is a powerful tool that can either reinforce stigma and solidify ethnic divisions or provide opportunities for tolerance and interethnic cooperation. If the inclusion of peace education curricula in Africa's schools, colleges, and universities has a potential to significantly reduce violence by influencing the youth to reject extremist ideology, partisan vitriol, and over-reliance on military solutions to address complex conflicts, teachers have to be taught "peace" themselves prior to teaching peace to students. In order to achieve this goal, two critical reforms have to occur: first, teachers need to engage in reflexivity that challenges their own views and biases. This may involve preservice and in-service training that enables continuous assessment of their influence and impact on peace and war curriculum, and second, reform the curriculum that at the moment overlooks opportunities for transformational peace that would allow young people to solve problems intelligently, diplomatically, and nonviolently.

RECOMMENDED READINGS

Ajirotutu, Cheryl. 2000. *African-Centered Schooling in Theory and Practice*. Westport: Bergin & Garvey.

Anne-Lynn, Dudenhoefer. 2016. *Understanding the Recruitment of Child Soldiers in Africa*. Mount Edgecombe, South Africa: African Center for the Constructive Resolution of Disputes.

Bodley-Bond, Carrie, and Karena Cronin. 2013. National Youth Service, Employability, Entrepreneurship and Sustainable Livelihoods: Overview of the National Youth Service Landscape in Sub-Saharan Africa (November). Johannesburg: South Africa.

Bratton, Michael. 2014. *Power Politics in Zimbabwe*. London: Lynne Rienner.

Panksepp, Jaak. 2012. *The Archaeology of Mind: Neuroevolutionary Origins of Human Emotions*. Washington, DC: W. W. Norton & Company.

Carter, Candice. 2015. *Social Education for Peace: Foundations, Teaching, and Curriculum for Visionary Learning*. London: Palgrave.

Carter, Charles. 2014. *Youth Literature for Peace Education*. London: Palgrave.

Chabal, Patrick, and Pascal Daloz. 1999. *Africa Works: Disorder as Political Instrument*. Oxford: James Currey.

Cunningham, Jeremy. 2015. *Conflict Transformation Through School: A Curriculum for Sustainable Peace*. London: Institute of Education.

Galtung, Johan. 2013. *More Than a Curriculum (Peace Education)*. Charlotte, N.C.: Information Age Publishing.

Guy, Arnold. 2009. *The A to Z of Civil Wars in Africa (The A to Z Guide Series)*. Lanham: Scarecrow Press.

King, Elizabeth. 2014. *From Classrooms to Conflict in Rwanda*. New York: Cambridge University.

Kisangani, Francois. 2012. *Civil Wars in the Democratic Republic of Congo*. London: Lynne Rienner.

Laia, Balcells. 2017. *Rivalry and Revenge: The Politics of Violence During Civil War*. Cambridge: Cambridge Studies.

Mac Ginty, Roger, and Oliver P. Richmond. 2013. "The Local Turn in Peace Building: A Critical Agenda for Peace." *Third World Quarterly* 34 (5):763–83.

Mbulakulima, Joel. 2017. *Introduce Peace, Conflict Resolution in Education Curriculum* (inaugural speech 22 June 2017). Lusaka: Zambia.

Metelits, Claire. 2016. *Security in Africa: A Critical Approach to Western Indicators of Threat*. London: Rowman & Littlefield.

Mufti, Emmanuel. 2012. *Teaching and Learning and the Curriculum: A Critical Introduction*. London: Bloomsbury.

Mutambara, Agrippa. 2014. *The Rebel in Me: A ZANLA Guerrilla Commander in the Rhodesian Bush War, 1974–1980*. Pinetown, South Africa: Helion & Company

Piazza, James. 2006. "Rooted in Poverty? Terrorism, Poor Economic Development, and Social Cleavages." *Terrorism and Political Violence* 18 (1):159–77.

Roessler, Philip. 2016. *Ethnic Politics and State Power in Africa: The Logic of the Coup-Civil War Trap*. Cambridge: Cambridge University.

Tahir-Ul-Qadri, Muhammad Islamic. 2015. *Curriculum on Peace and Counter-Terrorism: For Clerics, Imams and Teachers*. Lahore, Pakistan: Minhaj-ul-Quran.

Themnér, Anders. 2017. *Warlord Democrats in Africa: Ex-Military Leaders and Electoral Politics*. London: Zed Publishers.

The International Institute for Strategic Studies. 2017. *Armed Conflict Survey*. London

Uwazie, Enerst. 2003. *Conflict Resolution and Peace Education in Africa*. Boulder: Lexington.

Soro, Guillaume. 2015. *Why I Became a Rebel*. Yamoussoukro: Côte d'Ivoire.

Ward, Thomas. 1974. *Effective Learning: Lessons to Be Learned from Schooling*. East Lansing, MI: Michigan State University.

Decolonizing Practices for Western Educators

MICHELLE RIVERA-CLONCH

> Roses and garbage inter-are. Without a rose, we cannot have garbage; and without garbage, we cannot have a rose. They need each other very much. The rose and the garbage are equal. The garbage is just as precious as the rose. If we look deeply at the concepts of defilement and immaculateness, we return to the notion of inter-being.—Thich Nhat Hanh

Reading this passage from the engaged Buddhist text, *The Heart of Understanding*, I am struck by its attunement with the decolonizing practices of liberation psychology that are inherent, but not explicit, in its mytho-poetic language. Employing flowers and compost, Vietnamese monk and peace activist Thich Nhat Hanh highlights four decolonizing principles and practices from liberation psychology that are essential to a peace-centered classroom: multiplicity of perspectives; a systemic and contextual approach; power-sharing language; and anti-hierarchical values.

The two sister disciplines of liberation psychology and peace studies, which at first glance may look like separate and individual paradigms, have much in common to offer to a multilayered understanding of decolonization practices in peace-centered pedagogy. Collectively they espouse goals to identify mutual connections across perceived opposites; to help reduce rigid identification and polarizations; to increase tolerance for ambiguity, multiplicity, and change; to be iconoclastic by disrupting entrenched patterns; and promote participatory and engaged practices. What follows presents an outline of how to apply decolonizing practices from liberation psychology to peace-centered pedagogy and praxes.

According to Pacifica Graduate Institute, liberation psychology is broadly defined as "an orientation that seeks to develop and encourage local understandings and practices that can support people's desires and actions to create a more just, peaceful, and sustainable world." It also aims to reduce suffering at the individual, community, and collective levels. Ignacio Martín-Baró, a Spanish-born Jesuit and social psychologist working in El Salvador, first articulated it in the 1980s as a critical response to traditional Western psychologies. By embedding lived human experiences within a social and ideological state apparatus network, liberation psychologists work toward decentralizing the dominant individual psychological paradigm. In this way, individuals are encouraged to calibrate the weight distribution of injustice and accountability to include complex and intersecting systems, thereby reducing the onus of personalized burdens.

Engaged Buddhism teachings are included within this sub-discipline as it, too, is a critical response to a dominant spiritual paradigm. Like liberation psychologies and theologies, engaged Buddhism attends to the psycho-spiritual challenges, obstacles, and ruptures individuals may face alone or within communities. Therefore, liberation activist psychologists' writings and engaged Buddhism teachings represent this perspective.

L iberation psychology, as a critical response to dominating psychologies of the West, offers innovative perspectives with accompanying decolonizing practices for peace-centered pedagogy. Utilizing these practices provides Western educators with an opportunity to become aware of implicit bias toward Western theories, methodologies, and practices— particularly when engaging in cross-cultural or transnational teaching and training, collaborations, or research. Critical psychologists note this implicit bias as a "West is Best" approach to global south/north collaborations, and, for the purpose of peace-centered education, to the application of theoretical frameworks and pedagogical practices in the classroom. When this West is Best bias (implicit or not) is exported into the global south, it undermines local knowledges, methodologies, and wisdom and serves to reinforce intellectual colonization practices. With its focus on developing and supporting local knowledge production and implementation, as well as disrupting expert knowledges to honor multiple points of view, liberation psychology and its practices can enrich peace educators' planning and teaching processes.

Before proceeding, however, it is important to highlight the outline used to organize the remainder of this essay. Each of the first five lines of the above passage from Thich Nhat Hanh's *Heart of Understanding* are connected to one of four decolonizing principles and practices of liberation psychology. Thus, the opening line of the roses and garbage passage is our starting point.

Roses and garbage inter-are stresses the necessity of a multiplicity of perspectives in peace work. In this statement, Thich Nhat Hanh reminds us that roses have their own perspective on the world, and garbage has its own perspective on the world; they inter-are because one perspective cannot exist without the other. Similar to the viewer's experience when one studies the figure-ground image of the vase/two faces looking at each other, one realizes that one perspective is not more important than the other. Depending on the viewer's perspective or gaze, the background can shift to become the foreground and vice versa. Neither image disappears when one comes into focus; it is simply a shift in perspective and borders. Educators might be familiar with this inter-are concept through the work of Gestalt psychologists who promote the necessity of simultaneously being aware of the interplay between the object of focus, the foreground, and the context, or background, in an emergent situation.

If we extend this theoretical framework to trans- or cross-cultural education initiatives, we see how a multiplicity of viewpoints is crucial to decolonizing praxes. Basing their work on the writings of Brazilian educator Paulo Freire and liberation psychologist Ignacio Martin-Baro, Kathryn L. Norsworthy and Ouyporn Khuankaew "observed that those most negatively affected by powerful systems of domination have much to offer to struggles for social transformation; yet their voices tend to be the least heard and valued." Current educational and psychological models descending from Freire and Martin-Baro and rooted in liberation theory "center the voices of the poor and disenfranchized." By accessing voices and perspectives other than the dominant and patriarchal, individuals are encouraged to voice their own knowledge and wisdom as they reconstruct theories and create culturally relevant solutions to their own problems. Therefore, inclusion of multiple perspectives allows for students, classes, or communities to support each other as they deconstruct overgrown colonial structures and increase the psychic space of existing colonial narratives.

Particularly in cross-cultural educational settings and research, substantiating a single perspective as "the truth" is not helpful. To claim to have the truth instead entrenches binaries that often favor the dominant group and support exclusion. Just as the disenfranchized person's perspective is necessary to the struggle for liberation, a multiplicity of perspectives is central for culturally responsive education. Our role as educators invested in decolonizing educational practices requires that we model a deep understanding of perspective multiplicity by honoring the knowledge and voices of our students as well as the communities within which we work. This means we cannot dominate classroom time by enacting the "wise sage on the stage" role—the very thing for which many of us have been trained. It means that we must be willing to share the title of teacher with others in the room. It also means that we design curriculum with abundant opportunities to encourage and support the emergence of wisdom and problem solving of our students and local context. Being mindful of whose knowledge and solutions are acknowledged and implemented allows us to reduce the probability of coming in with a West is Best attitude—or unexamined vantage point—that actually undermines the learning possibilities at hand.

The second and third sentences of Thich Nhat Hanh's passage "without a rose we cannot have garbage; and without garbage we cannot have a rose. They need each other very much" point toward the centrality of systemic and contextual approaches in peace education. In their article, "Women of Burma Speak Out: Workshops to Deconstruct Gender-Based Violence and Build Systems of Peace and Justice," Norsworthy and Khuankaew describe a systemic and contextual approach as the foundation for their work. They maintain that understanding gender-based violence and forms of colonialism involves "recognizing the interlocking systems that support and preserve forms of oppression at the community, institutional, and structural levels." Marilyn Frye further supports this approach by suggesting that forms of oppression such as racism, classism, homophobia, and religious oppression, interconnect with sexism and misogyny to support and reinforce the subjugation of target groups. The tendencies for individuals to internalize, personalize, and de-contextualize their experiences from the cultural and societal levels are well known challenges in liberation initiatives. In an effort to interrupt the cycle of internalized oppression, liberation psychologists endeavor to offer a safe container for individuals to recognize that acts of colonialism, imperialism, and violence are embedded in an interconnected web of abusive systems that support power and privilege.

Fear of speaking truth to power, or feeling ashamed of what they perceive as their individual experience and inadequate response, individuals are often afraid to speak with others in their class, community, or with those who have authority to effect or alter their situation. This primarily happens because they do not wish to be stigmatized, ostracized, exiled, or made into a pariah for the group. When individuals are afraid, power-over dynamics by dominant groups are successfully maintained and re-inscribed. By effectively silencing individuals and groups, the dominant group feels able to publicly claim that there are no problems and that "the people" are content. Silencing individuals through threat, force, or fear publicly erases what are often shared experiences of suffering and trauma and forces affect, thoughts, and beliefs into the community underbelly. Just like us, students live within a social net wherein they enact various roles and responsibilities and are affected by the experiences of just and unjust systems and state institutions.

In nations where there is a history of intergenerational trauma such as occupation or colonialism, Stevens reminds us that speaking up against an authority figure or systems is remembered as and experienced as a dangerous act with potential material consequences—to their corporeality (torture, rape, isolation), property (seizure or destruction), and familial relations (separation, abduction, death). Disconnecting the personal from the political and invisibilizing it into the individual's psychic space is a very effective and age-old tactic of dominant groups; it is a straightforward divide-and-conquer methodology. As educators, we must consider the contexts, or background, from which our students arrive to the classroom. We must remain vigilant about the ways we might silence some of our students, how our classroom dynamics or other students might silence others, and how our text choices always bring forward certain voices while leaving others behind.

Peace-centered classrooms require examining the historical, cultural, and social context of an experience or event as a means to critically examine the grand narratives or proselytized truths of a culture. Including those who are invisible, at the margins, or at the borderlands of a society is necessary if the West is to transform its historical role of perpetuating a (unearned) privileged global north education. A systemic examination into how implicit bias—toward the global north and away from the global south—imbeds and interferes with professional pedagogy, practices, and research is needed. A self-reflexive examination into how implicit bias informs educational ethics, course materials selections, and interpersonal engagements is necessary in order for educators to avoid unintended yet insidious educational colonizing practices, particularly when working within a transnational model.

P ower-sharing language is the focus in the fourth sentence of the passage by Thich Nhat Hanh: "the rose and garbage are equal". One of the strategies used by those who wish to dominate and oppress is the control of rhetoric. Carefully chosen language, notes Spurr, can give the speaker a special role, power, or privilege, provide a sense of mastery over the other, affirm those who are needed to be allies, while at the same time debasing, classifying, negating, and unsubstantiating those viewed to be in a target group. In terms of colonization practices, Latina feminist Aurora Levins Morales posits that privileged language is used to silence and ridicule authentic stories, and invalidates individual voices based solely on language. She argues, "unnecessarily specialized language is used to humiliate those who are not supposed to feel entitled. It sells the illusion that only those who can wield it can think." Frantz Fanon, a postcolonial theorist who offers a critique of psychoanalysis, articulates this position most directly: "Every colonized people … finds itself face to face with the language of the civilizing nation," and, "the colonized is elevated above his jungle status in proportion to his adoption of the mother country's cultural standards." Peace-centered educators recognize the power of rhetoric and advocate for the use of power-sharing language in educational settings.

To intentionally use power-sharing language means to consciously work toward minimizing power-over dynamics in classroom relationships. To relieve the biased and dominant voice of the educator, decolonizing practices seek out and listen to multiple "languages" and perspectives. Not only does the educator avoid the role of omniscient expert and its corresponding jargon, but the educator also invites students to use holistic wisdom tools such as intuition, bodily knowledge, imagination, metaphors, and creative expression to engage the body and psyche as sources of knowledge. Providing a mix of experiential learning modalities increases students' self-awareness, interpersonal skills, and encourages a deeper integration of the concept of interdependence; all essential concepts to meaningful peace education. Creating space for these alternative languages helps to dethrone the privilege of intellectual and rational lectures of Western consciousness from reigning over pedagogical approaches and student learning.

Decolonizing the classroom requires an increased awareness of the varying power differentials in the room, how these differentials are represented through the instructional language we choose, the language students use to articulate their questions and wisdom, and encourages teachers, peer facilitators, and students to engage in collaborative and productive partnerships. The use of power-sharing language offers the real possibility that one perspective is not privileged or given power-over the multitude of "Other" and valid perspectives.

The next sentence of Thich Nhat Hanh's passage, "the garbage is just as precious as the rose", highlights anti-hierarchical values. Particularly in global south/north courses, trainings, or workshops, Western educators must remain vigilant about not applying power-over dynamics, as it does not encourage honest sharing, dialogue, and creativity. If hierarchical West is Best values are covertly present in classroom settings or embedded in research design, colonization practices materialize. Bringing West is Best hierarchy bias into research and the classroom signals a historical colonial subtext wherein the procedural object is to conquer, divide, and manipulate the subordinate group. According to Freire, to conquer is to possess, personalize, or reduce another's status. To divide is to isolate, de-unify, and act to preserve the status quo. To manipulate is to conform, create unauthentic organization, and anesthetize the very people we aim to help. Educators must be mindful about how international identity location, social capital, and professional influence operate in contexts different than one's own.

To this end, it behooves peace-centered educators to develop a critical consciousness in their own work and in their work with others. One strategy is to have students engage course content at the heart level by reflecting on a learning experience through affect (for example how was that experience for you? How did it make you feel?); to engage at the head level by analyzing what they learned from the experience (what did you learn as an individual?); communicating and harvesting new learnings at the group level through large group discussions (what did we learn here as a group? Which connections are you making?), and engaging at the hand level by applying the new learnings from the classroom to transform elements of oppression and domination in their own lives and/or in their local communities. Norsworthy and Khuankaew note that this process helps everyone involved—teacher and student—to develop heightened critical consciousness and for all to take responsibility for social change. Students do well to support each other in this consciousness-raising process by processing their learning experiences together in an anti-hierarchical group structure. Benefits include increasing solidarity among individual members, normalizing experiences and feelings of group members, universalizing experiences and feelings by relating them to contexts and systems, and accruing empathic understanding toward oneself and others.

Freire provides an excellent example of when the presence of an ego-centric, hierarchical self diminishes a teaching and learning experience for everyone. He writes, "The antidialogical, dominating *I* transforms the dominated, conquered *thou* into a mere *it.*" As such, peace-centered ontology and values do not support approaching pedagogical experiences with a simple reliance on hierarchical logic such as single-coursed expertise, reductionism, fixed ideas, linearity, and verticality.

P eace-centered educators are encouraged to seek out anti-hierarchical structures to work within or to create themselves. To work in solidarity with local peoples, we need to especially pay attention to the areas in which our Western eyes and ears may not be well trained to pay attention. When we engage in anti-hierarchical methodologies and do not privilege what we, as Westerners, feel is most important in any given situation, we create a trusting and fertile learning environment for our students. It is not that we do not consider the wisdom of the West when working across borders; we are mindful to not automatically privilege it or to have it erase other possibilities.

If we look deeply at the concepts of defilement and immaculateness, we return to the notion of inter-being, and following Thich Nhat Hanh's lead, we come full circle to conclusion. The interconnected disciplines of liberation psychology and peace education collectively espouse goals to identify shared connections; help reduce rigid identification; increase capacity for ambiguity, multiplicities, and change; to be iconoclastic; and to be participatory in nature. They are uniquely situated in relation to one another and have an inherent responsibility to lend support to their respective concerns. In this spirit, liberation psychology offers Western educators examples of how to expand the scope of pedagogical approaches, classroom instruction, and research design to include peace-centered methodologies. Accordingly, this essay began with the mytho-poetic idea that if roses and garbage inter-are, then a non-dualistic approach is needed to support optimal learning in the classroom. A systemic and contextual approach, where without garbage we cannot have a rose and without a rose we cannot have garbage, increases the effectiveness of peace-centered pedagogies. Both disciplines face the challenge of decentralizing dominant voices in order to express alternatives, share private burdens, and harvest the private to the public. Since the rose and garbage are theoretically equal, iconoclastic discourses found in liberation psychology and peace education emphasize the necessity of power-sharing language. Finally, shared anti-hierarchal values and methodologies eloquently affirm that the putrid and shadowy chaos of garbage is just as precious as the tender beauty and radiance of a rose.

Whether Western educators are in the classroom or out in the field, they can align their pedagogical process with their peace-centered instruction by using decolonizing practices as outlined by liberation psychology. When we intentionally bring this alignment into our classroom, we walk our talk and increase our credibility and effectiveness with students. It is imperative that Western educators, who are often in positions of power and influence, are constantly raising their own consciousness and that of their colleagues around their global north identity. Without this, West is Best implicit bias erodes and undermines the potential for transformative classroom experiences. We have much to learn from our students, we only need to be willing to listen, not be too eager to fix, seek out marginalized voices, and respectfully incorporate their wisdom and contributions into the learning environment of our classrooms.

RECOMMENDED READINGS

Clarkson, Petruska. 2004. *Gestalt Counseling in Action*. 3rd ed. London, UK: Sage.
Cone, James H. 1989. *Black Theology and Black Power*. New York, NY: Orbis.
Fanon, Franz. 1967. *Black Skin: White Masks*. New York, NY: Grove Press.
Freire, Paulo. 1972. *Pedagogy of the Oppressed*. New York, NY: Herder & Herder.
Frye, Marilyn. 2016. "Oppression." In *Race, Class, and Gender in the United States*, edited by P.S. Rothenberg, 130–33, 10th ed. New York, NY: Worth Publishers.
King, Martin L. 1968. *Where Do We Go from Here: Chaos or Community?* Boston: Beacon.

Martin-Baro, Ignacio. 1994. *Writings for a Liberation Psychology*. Cambridge, MA: Harvard University Press.

Morales, Aurora L. 1998. *Medicine Stories: History, Culture, and the Politics of Integrity*. Cambridge, MA: South End Press.

Nhat Hanh, Thich. 1988. *The Heart of Understanding*. Berkeley, CA: Parallax Press.

Norsworthy, Kathryn L. and Ouyporn Khuankaew. 2004. "Women of Burma Speak Out: Workshops to Deconstruct Gender-Based Violence and Build Systems of Peace and Justice." *Journal for Specialists in Group Work* 29 (3):259–83.

Pacifica Graduate Institute 2017. Liberation Psychology. Accessed July 26, 2017. <https://www.pacifica.edu/degree-program/community-liberation-ecopsychology/liberation-psychology/>.

Perls, Fritz. 1992. *Gestalt Therapy Berbatim*. Gouldsboro, ME: Gestalt Journal Press.

Prilleltensky, Isaac, and Geoffrey Nelson. 2002. *Doing Psychology Critically: Making a Difference in Diverse Settings*. New York, NY: Palgrave.

Shulman, Helene, and Mary Watkins. 2010. *Toward Psychologies of Liberation*. New York, NY: Palgrave.

Spurr, David. 1996. *The Rhetoric of Empire: Colonial Discourse in Journalism, Travel Writing, and Imperial Administration*. Durham, NC: Duke University Press.

Stevens, Maurice E. 2014. "Before After Catastrophe." *Oppositional Conversations* 1 (2). Accessed August 20, 2017. <http://cargocollective.com/OppositionalConversations_Iii/Before-AfterCatastrophe>.

Tutu, Desmond M. 1999. *No Future without Forgiveness*. New York, NY: Random House.

Teaching Peace, Not War, to U.S. History Students

Timothy Braatz

In a war-making society, teaching peace as a rejection of war requires boldness—a characteristic, in my experience, not typically found in history instructors at work. While the field of peace studies overtly rejects violence in all its forms (hopefully), historians tend to claim or aspire to academic detachment or objectivity. But "you can't be neutral on a moving train," historian Howard Zinn taught us, and the "train" of U.S. history, as engineered by the dominant opinion-pushers, celebrates and euphemizes war.

In U.S. colleges and universities, students typically enter history classrooms knowing next to nothing about history but believing in the general goodness and necessity of U.S. war-making. For most, this is an unexamined assumption, a received truth. They have been convinced—by schoolteachers, family members, Hollywood films, ministers, corporate news reporters, popular literature, national holidays, military recruitment ads, sporting events pageantry—that war brought freedom from England, abolished slavery, civilized North America, simultaneously ended the Holocaust and Great Depression, blocked the spread of evil Communism, and currently protects U.S. citizens from terrorism. Neatly put, "our servicemen and women defend our freedoms." What's not to like?

History professors are uniquely positioned to shape opinions on war. They generally enjoy academic freedom (not to be taken for granted) and a classroom authority that goes mostly unchallenged (for better or worse) by a somewhat captive and submissive audience (grades!). History professors typically are experienced researchers, know the value of primary sources, and have sufficient time to construct compelling, evidence-based arguments (as opposed to spewing sound bites). Despite the ongoing devaluation of liberal education, a quarter of public institutions still require students to complete at least one broad survey course in U.S.

history or government. Finally, unlike colleagues in other social sciences and humanities, historians are tasked with maintaining a broad narrative of the past, and in the U.S. past, warfare is a major theme. These privileges have allowed the history professorate, more often than not, to perpetuate war worship (mostly through uncritical storytelling), but can also be used to promote war skepticism.

The effort must be outright—half measures will not do, not against deeply engrained assumptions—and the time to start is now. Human society is in a state of upheaval—extreme climate change, vicious oil markets, expanding population, declining U.S. empire, dying oceans—and massively armed with weapons of war. Teachers should weigh this moral equation: The U.S. military state is the leading war-making institution, only U.S. popular opinion and nonviolent resistance have the power to stop the war machine, and teachers help shape popular opinion. A history curriculum that does not encourage students to ask critical questions about war-making is part of the problem. Which side are you on?

So you would like to do your part, you would like to use your U.S. history class (or related field) to teach peace and reject war, you are even willing to risk pressure from administrators and public harassment from ideological provocateurs. But you have an obligation to fulfill the official course outline and also want to remain true to the ideals of free inquiry. Perfect. Your task is not to convert your students into antiwar activists—attempting that will cost you your audience. Rather, your task is to raise critical questions, provide non-celebratory analyses, and encourage students to think for themselves. This may seem obvious in theory, but in practice is a radical endeavor. Try it and see. Some general principles will help:

First, be transparent. State your biases as they shape your teaching—preferably on Day 1. This is an effective way to introduce students to the subjectivity of history-telling. Students have learned that biased means unfair and dishonest. But a bias is simply an interest, and everyone has interests, and your interests influence the choices you make as an instructor, such as what to include or exclude from your lessons. In this context, announcing that you ardently reject all war or that you embrace nonviolence is not preaching but, rather, full disclosure and pedagogically sound. Students, even those with contrary interests, will appreciate the honesty. Some might be inspired.

Second emphasize perspective. This follows quickly from a discussion on bias. Ten witnesses to a traffic accident will give you ten different accounts. Thus, we must consider from whose perspective a story is being told. Establishing the principle of perspective will justify an examination

TEACHING PEACE AND WAR

of a given war from multiple viewpoints—soldiers, families of soldiers, noncombatants in war zones, laborers in munitions factories, prisoners, and others. War is miserable for almost all involved—choose primary documents, especially firsthand accounts, to demonstrate this.

Third teach critical thinking. Professional educators love to talk about critical thinking but few genuinely promote it (so many educationalists, so few teachers). The stifling of critical thought typically begins on Day 1 of a college course, with the presentation of a lengthy syllabus containing the instructor's objectives, a precise schedule of topics, and "student learning outcomes." The superficial message is "This is how our class will proceed." The deeper message is "I'm the expert, I know what you need to know, I control what you will learn."

Since the military state requires a passive, gullible citizenry, empowering students is an act of resistance. Maybe begin Day 1 by asking, "What do you want to learn?" Expect confused silence. Most students have never encountered this question; they are waiting for you to explicate what matters most: grading formula and exam format; they are well trained. So next ask, gently, how it is that they are so passive and cowed. Most know, deep down, that much of their education has been dictatorial, coercive, fundamentalist. Encouraged to reflect on this, they will warm to the task. Critical thinking has begun.

Fourth, apply critical thought to traditional history-telling. When faced with a story, four simple questions are useful: Is it true? How do you know it's true? Why are you telling me this? What are you leaving out? Most students ask some version of these questions when faced with schoolyard rumors but passively accept the authority of teachers, textbooks, and televised talking heads.

Take a story from your standard curriculum, perhaps the so-called Boston Massacre, and apply the questions. First: Is it true that British soldiers massacred Boston colonists in 1770? Turns out, this "massacre" was a complicated mob scene resulting in five deaths. Second: How do we know it's true? This is a call for evidence—primary documents—and a variety of eyewitness accounts are available, with the expected inconsistencies. Third: Why is the "massacre" a standard piece of U.S. history curriculum? Put another way, what's the implied message of this story as taught to schoolchildren? That's obvious, once someone shows you: The British soldiers murdered innocent American colonists, thus British soldiers were perpetrators, Americans were victims, and the Independence War was a necessary and successful exercise in good overcoming evil. Fourth: What gets left out?

In using this arguably minor event to provide context for a war supposedly about colonial freedom versus British tyranny, history teachers might fail to mention how the war was also shaped by internal class conflict (colonial elites repressing a revolution) and the issue of slavery (with the British as antislavery forces). When you read how officers in the Continental Army mistreated enlisted men, and how slaves were fleeing to British lines, the glory of the "American Revolution" fades. You might also examine how the people of Canada and India gained independence from British rule without warring against it.

Warning: Students might apply the four critical questions to your own assertions. If you believe in free inquiry, you must be open to criticism. Encourage it. See "Be Transparent" above.

Fifth, always tie past to present. Studying history prepares us to analyze and correct current injustices. History does not repeat itself, not in a literal sense, but we can identify and learn from historical trends, patterns, systems, and behaviors. A critical approach to standard curricula will provide many opportunities to challenge the assumptions behind pro-war thinking, then and now. For example, in a lesson on the Boston "massacre," featuring Sam Adams and Paul Revere, you can discuss how opinion-pushers use inflammatory propaganda and victimhood (see the Alamo, *U.S.S. Maine*, Bay of Tonkin, 9/11) to justify war-making, how traditional U.S. history-telling encourages students to view the world from a nationalist (USA versus them) perspective rather than through a lens of, say, economic class (rich versus poor) or human rights (slavery versus antislavery). You might evaluate the notion that USA equals freedom.

Bonus: Students are quickly bored by a recitation of names and dates. They are more engaged when they discover that historical knowledge is empowering and that history is a constantly evolving discussion over what is worth remembering and how it should be remembered. Critical history makes history class critical.

Sixth, reject nationalist language, particularly the nationalist "we." Historical inquiry means asking who did what. Precise language is important. Encourage your students to be as specific as possible in naming historical actors. For example, do not use "America" as a historical agent, as in "America fought with England" or "America wanted to stop Hitler." "America" is an abstraction, an idea, not an entity that thinks, acts, and feels. Misuse of this term perpetuates the fallacy that the U.S. population is united and single-minded, including on questions of war.

Similarly, do not apply "we" to things you were not involved in. "We invaded Vietnam" and similar phrases conceal more than they enlighten. Who actually invaded Vietnam? Who made the decisions and who opposed them? What were their motives? Is there a similarity between such war decisions then and now? Like "America," the nationalist "we" causes students to equate themselves with U.S. policy makers and the U.S. military, to assume a national unity that never has existed. Deconstructing nationalist language opens the mind to more careful thinking, perhaps leading to the conclusion that U.S. war-makers do not represent the interests and desires of the U.S. population in general.

Seventh, be alert to language that depicts war as inevitable, natural, or accidental. Again, this is a question of precision. The obvious error is to state outright that "the war was inevitable" or "there was no way to avoid war." Other examples are more subtle. Passive voice phrasing—"The young men were drafted"; "The city was bombed"—often omits the decision-makers and perpetrators. Making warfare the active subject of the sentence can have a similar effect: "War broke out"; "Hostilities ensued." Check student papers, and your own lectures, for such grammatical laziness. Instead of "An atomic bomb was dropped on Hiroshima," insist on "With President Truman's approval, a U.S. Army pilot dropped an atomic bomb on Hiroshima." War-making is always a choice.

Eighth, do not sanitize slaughter. Reject euphemisms and call war what it is. War is slaughter, not a sporting event, and almost everyone involved suffers greatly. When students speak of "winning" a war, introduce Jeanette Rankin and ask them to evaluate her claim that "You can no more win a war than you can win an earthquake." Employ phrases like "World Slaughter One" and "the Iraq Slaughter" and see how they alter the conversation. Emphasize the human and environmental toll of warfare. Provide firsthand accounts of suffering. Show explicit photographs. "With President Truman's approval, a U.S. Army pilot dropped an atomic bomb on Hiroshima, a city of Japanese families, slaughtering tens of thousands instantly. Now let's look at some pictures of the immediate devastation and long-term consequences."

Ninth, include the suffering of U.S. citizens. When you ask critical questions about U.S. war-making, some students will assume you are denigrating U.S. military personnel in general. They may be military veterans themselves, come from military families, or romanticize military service from a safe distance (the latter category is of greatest concern). You will begin to win their sympathy, however, when you discuss how the average combat soldier is underpaid, exploited, and traumatized; how war planners put enlistees in dangerous situations, order them to kill or be killed, then discard them. For most students, war is something that happens far away, to someone else, and might even be "good for the economy." A discussion of historical U.S. war-making is incomplete without examination of the cost at home—disrupted families, posttraumatic stress disorder and domestic violence, reduced budgets for schools and other public services, environmental pollution including nuclear waste, and compromised democracy. If students have previously encountered heart-warming stories of "America at War," ask them to apply the critical questions: Why did my instructor emphasize "Rosie the Riveter"? What did she leave out?

Tenth, explain nonviolence. The principles listed above promote critical examination of war-making, and students will ultimately agree that warfare is awful. Lacking awareness of better options, however, they will still imagine such slaughter is a necessary evil. By introducing historical examples of nonviolence, you can suggest alternatives to violent conflict resolution and ways to resist war-makers. But first you have to explain the dynamics of nonviolence (which means you need to learn them). The Civil Rights Movement is a good place to start—indeed, it can be the centerpiece of a U.S. history survey course, as it nonviolently transformed society in numerous ways. Regarding the Movement, students typically know Martin Luther King Jr. had a dream and has a holiday, they know Rosa Parks remained seated, and little else. They have never heard of, for example, Diane Nash, John Lewis, or James Lawson. They do not know how nonviolence works. This is your big moment—where peace studies and U.S. history conspicuously overlap—make the most of it! Teach peace!

And do not stop there. The Civil Rights Movement contributed to an antiwar movement, which pressured U.S. officials to abandon the destruction of Vietnam and, later, awakened U.S. citizens to the dangers of nuclear arsenals and kept U.S. officials from all-out war against the people of Nicaragua. Highlight nonviolent acts of resistance, including by U.S. military personnel and veterans.

The end of the Cold War affords another great opportunity to teach peace. Some students will have heard that "Reagan won the Cold War" by expanding the military budget. Examine the evidence: Did Soviet spending increases follow U.S. increases? What inspired Gorbachev to reform the Soviet Union? (Hint: It had more to do with Steve Jobs than with Reagan). While Reagan was "winning," what were U.S. citizens losing? Most of all, what was the role of nonviolent movements in dismantling dictatorships in central Europe?

High school history instructors typically must cover a strict agenda of historical events and themes and may have no input on textbook choices. College professors have much greater academic freedom but still have obligations to catalog descriptions, particularly in survey courses. By adhering to the above principles, history teachers at all levels can present the required curriculum and still teach peace by introducing students to nonviolence while exposing war for the collective disaster that it is. Your contribution may seem trivial, but a big peace is made up of lots of little pieces.

What to do about the special case of World War II? The problem, simply put, is that U.S. opinion-pushers (pundits, politicians, filmmakers, teachers, et al.) love it. In general, they are conflicted about the destruction of Vietnam and Iraq, uninterested in the failure of U.S. forces to conquer the Korean peninsula and (currently) Afghanistan, uninspired by World War I, and ignorant of how U.S. forces violently subjugated Mexico, the Philippines, and the Caribbean. U.S. participation in World War II, though, is easily depicted as heroic, righteous, and triumphant—the "Good War"— and your students will carry these assumptions. Therein lies a great opportunity to promote war skepticism, as World War II is a major event in U.S. history, students are intrigued by the topic, the U.S. "victory" is used to justify current U.S. militarism, and countering the pervasive celebratory history will require you to examine your own assumptions (always a good practice). The discussion that follows might be useful.

A teacher may be expected to cover a timeline of World War II events, but there are different ways to frame this. One approach is to emphasize historical memory by beginning with a question—Why is World War II still so prominent, even beloved, in U.S. culture, especially compared to other wars? Identify the key reasons, then apply the principles listed above and see how the story changes. Here are some examples:

They started it. Unlike the rest of U.S. war-making since 1865, the U.S. military state is not the clear aggressor in World War II. This is the usual starting point—"America" as victim, fighting a defensive, justified war. The simple narrative is that the Japanese military attacked Pearl Harbor (1941), and, after the U.S. Congress defensively declared war on Japan, the German government declared war on the United States. To provide a different context, start your narrative decades earlier, with U.S. forces establishing a Pacific empire from California to the Philippines. When Japanese forces began colonizing the western Pacific, in the 1930s, U.S. officials responded with threats and economic sanctions. The Pearl Harbor attack did not "come out of nowhere"; this was a conflict between two expanding empires. Perhaps invoke the perspective of Filipinos: over 300 years of Spanish occupation and exploitation, then brutal conquest by U.S forces, then violent Japanese invasion.

We won. The German and Japanese military states surrendered to the U.S. military state. Case closed … unless one deconstructs the language. Who is the "we" and what did they "win"? What was the cost to U.S. civilians and military personnel (including those of Japanese descent)? How can anyone speak of "winning" with over sixty million killed around the globe? Forget nationalist categories—humanity lost. Also, consider how this "victory" contributed to the creation of the permanent U.S. military state and led directly to the Korean War. The standard, celebratory version of U.S. participation in World War II, from Pearl Harbor to V-J Day, is neat, a clear beginning and end. With broader historical context, a different truth emerges: one war leads to another. Rather than discrete events, wars are better understood collectively as a societal disease in need of a cure.

Good versus Evil. The celebratory version is not only neat, it's a morality tale. The villains are Hitler (the personification of evil in the Western imagination), the Nazis (as distinguished from "good Germans"), and "Japs" (genetically subhuman, no distinctions necessary). The heroes are U.S. military personnel (with a nod to British allies) opposing evil, thus, by definition, virtuous. Fine ... until you examine how U.S. and British technicians carefully planned the bombing of German cities to maximize civilians deaths; how Truman's approval of nuclear bombing was a political, not military, decision. If you decry the slaughter of civilians as wicked, then respond with your own slaughter of civilians, what does that make you? The role of the Soviet Army ("good" Americans allied with "evil" Communists?) further undermines the simple morality formulation.

Against Fascism. Fascism is bad, and U.S. forces were fighting to stop its spread. Sounds heroic, but is it true? Begin with a definition of fascism. Celebratory history requires a strict definition, including dictatorship and worship of the state, to disqualify the U.S. political system. What happens, though, if you present a list of the characteristics of a fascist system, including corporation–state alliance, repression of dissent, anti-Marxism and hostility to labor rights, imperialism, militarism, extreme nationalism, and state-enforced sexism and racism? Were U.S. officials and citizens opposed to such practices and beliefs in the years before and during World War II? While we are on the subject, students, what about today?

Ending the Holocaust. British and U.S. forces defeated the Nazis, thereby saving untold numbers of Jews (and others). Without U.S. violent intervention, the destruction of European Jews would have been complete. How can one argue with that? The first point to raise is that the liberation of concentration camps, by Soviet and Western forces, was an accidental byproduct of war, never a stated goal. Indeed, U.S. officials passed on several opportunities to save European Jews from Nazi persecution. Second, ask students to use their imaginations. Instead of assuming that warfare is the only way to counter a genocidal regime, can we envision a nonviolent response? Students will scoff—nonviolent resistance to Nazis?—until you present the examples: Le Chambon and Rosenstrasse, Denmark, and Norway—the latter three spontaneous and untrained. What might well-funded and well-trained nonviolent civilian defense accomplish? How about an international *shanti sena* (nonviolent intervention force)? Rather than fighting evil with evil, thus propagating the disease, a cure may be available. Revisiting the past opens possibilities for the future.

To summarize, by asking critical questions of celebratory accounts of war-making in U.S. history, a history curriculum can undermine war worship and promote creative, nonviolent conflict resolution. Peace.

RECOMMENDED READINGS

Alperovitz, Gar. 1995. *The Decision to Use the Atomic Bomb*. New York: Knopf.

Braatz, Timothy. 2015. *Peace Lessons*. Minneapolis: Disproportionate Press.

Braatz, Timothy. 2015. "Speaking of War." *Peace Review* 27 (3):371–8.

Costs of War Project, Watson Institute, Brown University. watson.brown.edu/costsofwar/.

Dower, John. 1986. *War Without Mercy: Race and Power in the Pacific War*. New York: Pantheon.

Friedrich, Jörg. 2006. *The Fire: The Bombing of Germany, 1940–1945*. New York: Columbia University Press.

Postman, Neil, and Charles Weingartner. 1969. *Teaching as a Subversive Activity*. New York: Dell.

Swanson, David. 2016. War is Never Just. davidswanson.org.

War and Peace in Iraqi Kurdistan's History Curricula

MARWAN DARWEISH AND MAAMOON ALSAYID MOHAMMED

Since its inception in 2003, Kurdistan's Regional Government (KRG) has implemented a wide range of reforms in Iraqi Kurdistan's (IK) education system. The history education curricula (HEC) students encounter glorify war, exclude different narratives or interpretations, and fail to foster critical debate or enquiry. In their explicit content, as well as in their implications, processes, and delivery, IK's HEC encourage violence, foster divisions between Muslims and non-Muslims, and serve to establish the dominance of the most powerful group in society.

International law does not recognize Kurdistan as a defined area, although its de facto borders are acknowledged by the Kurdish people. Estimates suggest that there are 20 to 40 million Kurds in the world, with about four million living in Iraq; the majority are Sunni Muslims, and the remainder includes Shiia, Assyrian, and Yezidi minorities. Three main dialects are spoken in Iraqi Kurdistan and these differences, as well as geographical and political divisions, have been key factors in the failure of Kurds to establish autonomy and any cohesive sense of identity. Continual divisions and rivalry between Shiia and Sunni groups in Iraq and IK have helped to ethnicize the education system: when Sunni factions held power and decisions about education were made in Baghdad, history curricula promoted Ba'athist values and ideology. Under self-rule, HEC are being used to promote Kurdish national identity.

Iraq is, unofficially, divided into three demographically and ethnically separate parts, with Kurds in the north, Sunni Arabs in the middle, and Shiia in the south. IK in the oil-rich north is a de facto state thanks to its military and economic power, and although its resources have been reduced by war with Islamic State forces and its support for the basic needs of Syrian refugees and internally displaced Iraqi people, its strategic importance has created the opportunity for the historically disadvantaged Kurds to contemplate independence. The IK voted overwhelmingly in favor of independence in a non-binding referendum on September 25, 2017.

The KRG's growing confidence is evident in its work to develop HEC free from Baghdad's influence that reflect the aspirations, identity, and history of the Kurdish people; however, these HEC do little to integrate and disseminate knowledge, values, and skills that support peace. Instead, IK's HEC contribute to the marginalization and delegitimization of other ethnic groups and to the consolidation of the dominant group's authority.

Although there is no consensus about how to define Peace Education, it is generally agreed that, first, it should be context-specific; second, that it should involve the promotion of knowledge, skills, and values that prevent direct, cultural, and structural violence, and third, that it should build peaceful relations at all levels. It can be used to encourage reflection on the past and transformation and positive change at individual levels and beyond. Conversely, particularly when a society is in flux, History Education (HE) can serve to legitimize the dominant group's existence and justify certain acts, behavior, and attitudes. It can also facilitate the kinds of state-building work being undertaken by the KRG.

Since 1991, when the IK education system was reformed in line with a nationalist grand narrative that involved the "Kurdification" of HE textbooks, the narratives of other religious and ethnic groups have been repressed or manipulated in HEC in ways that aggravate intergroup hostility in a diverse, multiethnic society. Our study of IK's history textbooks for pupils in grades five to eight (ages 11–14) is based on research conducted in public schools in Duhok, Erbil, and Sulaimaniyah in 2013 and 2014. We observed classes, examined textbooks, and interviewed teachers, curricula developers, policy makers, teacher-trainers, and pupils, among others. We also coordinated a focus group with other parties including policy influencers, parents, and students.

We found that IK's history textbooks foreground the Kurds' national aspirations. Ancient Kurdistan is represented as a large state that extended from the Zakros Mountains to the northeast of Mesopotamia, and Kirkuk is presented as being under the jurisdiction of the KRG, rather than an independent city. The textbooks state that Kurds have fought for self-determination as well as cultural and democratic rights throughout history. They also suggest that the host governments of Iraq, Iran, Turkey, and Syria have refused to respond peacefully, instead using violence to annihilate the Kurds and to provoke the independence struggle. The Iraqi government regards the Kurds as an overambitious minority group, while

Kurds believe they are an occupied nation, denied their territorial rights and natural resources.

Since self-rule began in 1991, school curricula have taught students loyalty to their homeland of Kurdistan, which is represented as including oil-rich Kirkuk as well as the three provinces of Duhok, Erbil, and Sulaimaniyah. Schools deliver curricula through the Kurdish language, with English as the second language. Only a few Arabic-speaking schools are dedicated to internally displaced Arabs from elsewhere in Iraq, so young people in Kurdistan do not speak Arabic nor do they consider themselves to be Iraqis.

History Education (HE) textbooks explain that the international community fragmented Kurdish society between states after World War I. In focusing on the fight for Kurdish rights after the emergence of the Iraqi State, they present a picture of demoralization and powerlessness and engender distrust of the international community and Iraqi government. Students are encouraged to yearn for an idealized past, without engaging with current realities. The Islamic State (662 CE–750 CE) is described as having been powerful and effective in ensuring equality, freedom, and justice for all of its citizens; Kurdistan is always mentioned as being separate from an Iraq that Kurds never wanted to be a part of; and cooperation with the Iraqi government is represented as an always unsuccessful strategy. HE textbooks have effectively facilitated the construction of national consciousness and identity based around the idea of a "great Kurdistan," encompassing all of the places where Kurds live.

Teachers impart the prepackaged history curriculum in good faith to students who believe that it transmits truth. This transfer occurs within a culture where a "successful school" is expected to deliver volumes of information to students who internalize it along with the principle of submission, not only to teachers but to course content that is avowedly warlike. HE textbooks suggest that it was through wars that empires gained territories, states gained self-determination, and resources became secure. No opportunity is provided for students to become critical of these views or to develop different interpretations. Only one narrative is promulgated, and opportunities for discussion are not embedded in course delivery.

Textbooks criticize wars in the pre-Islamic period, which they suggest were waged without justification. Meanwhile, wars waged under Islam are represented as legitimate efforts to spread the faith. The Prophet referred to nonviolent Jihad as being more important than its violent counterpart. Most of the teachers we interviewed agreed that Jihad has various nonviolent meanings, but HE textbooks conceptualize Jihad in terms of violence rather than the pursuit of personal purity.

Textbooks claim that the state can justify war to achieve the expansion of territory, the liberation of occupied areas, access to resources, deterrence, or self-defense, but students are not being equipped to think critically, to discuss the justification for wars, or to think about the relevance of the international humanitarian laws that govern them. The textbooks suggest that truly effective approaches to conflict resolution are based on force and power, and that peace can only be secured if states prepare for war and increase their military capability. Muslims emerge as winners over defeated nonbelievers or non-Muslims even in defeat because their fighters (*peshmergah*) are represented as martyrs for their religion and country. Students are shown that, even where peace is obtained, it is won thanks to enforcement and "power over" the other rather than "power with" the other (or "peace through strength").

Iraqi Kurdistan's HEC are silent about peaceful resolutions or education for peace, except when they refer to the constitution the Prophet Mohammed established in Madinah. Beyond mention of this agreement, which called for cooperation and peaceful conflict resolution between Muslims and non-Muslims, HEC textbooks teach that states declare war in order to instill beliefs and impose culture on others by forcing the religion of Islam on non-Muslims. For example, IK's fifth-year textbook mentions the war that Abu Bakir and other *Caliphs* carried out against groups dissenting from Islam after the Prophet's death. The textbooks ignore the conditions that led to this dissent, its meaning, implications, and its potential applicability to contemporary Kurdish history and politics. IK's HEC imply that the use of violence is justified in such cases and so contradict their basic human right to exercise freedom of choice. Yet, when Muslims are shown to have been prevented from practicing their religion by the Quraish tribe, they are described as having been wrongly persecuted. At moments like these, IK's HEC overlook their own contradictions and sideline issues that might usefully cast light on contemporary issues in Iraqi Kurdistan.

The establishment of the Islamic State and the use of war to spread Islam are classed, without question, as forms of liberation, and the defense of one's state by all means possible is presented as something valuable and as a source of pride. Iraqi Kurdistan's HE textbooks insist that all means should be used to maximize harm to the other side in a conflict situation, and the destruction of people's belongings, property, and lives are not assessed in relation to international humanitarian standards.

IK's HEC never link information about past wars with current conflicts in the Middle East or elsewhere. Students consume simple descriptions and narratives of events that exclude mention of the international community and third-party interventions for peacemaking and post-conflict reconstruction; they are never asked to consider the role of the United Nations or regional bodies in preventing violence, providing peacekeeping missions, or mediating and resolving conflicts.

Overall, IK's history textbooks promote warlike values rather than explore peace; even peaceful demonstrations are described as having been legitimately curbed by violent means. The idea that peace has only ever been achieved through violence helps legitimize its continued use in contemporary IK and Iraq. Our research interviews suggest that classroom delivery does little to temper this message. As one teacher explained, "we want to teach our students that the blessed life that they are in, did not come in vaguely, without sacrifices. KRG made a lot of sacrifices, martyrs, without *peshmergah* we would not be in this situation. These students have seen nothing, no wars, no sufferings, and it is good to be reminded from time to time."

When HE textbooks do discuss peaceful and constructive ways to resolve conflict, they focus on solutions that emerge from Islamic history and teachings. They explain, for example, that the Prophet Mohammed used conflict management techniques to evade war with the Quraish tribe and they discuss formal, informal, traditional, and religious methods of arbitration, widely accepted as a method of resolving conflict in most Muslim countries and in the Quran. Yet, even when a "diplomatic way" to approach non-Muslims about paying taxes according to Islamic law is discussed, the implicit message is that non-Muslims must cooperate with the state or face punishment.

Reconciliation, presented as another peaceful approach to conflict, is explained via information about the Prophet initiating *Sulh Alhudaibia* as an agreement of reconciliation with the Quraish tribe. The story, however briefly related, demonstrates that the Prophet preferred peace to war, but the textbooks highlight neither the conditions that led to the agreement, nor the fact that the interests and needs of the other party were met to facilitate it. The Prophet also negotiated with the Quraish to allow people who resigned from Islam to return to their tribe, but this fact is not used to open discussion about the right of religious affiliation or conflict resolution in contemporary Kurdistan. Instead, reconciliation tends to be presented as the last recourse of the weaker side, or as a means to buy time or deceive others. In this way, HE textbooks reflect Kurdistan's prevailing social and cultural norms, which stigmatize as weak anyone who attempts reconciliation or makes concessions.

Martyrdom, meanwhile, is celebrated repeatedly as a show of strength. HEC textbooks conceptualize martyrdom as a Muslim way of sacrificing oneself for the sake of one's religion and/or nation. Although the concept of martyrdom is mentioned in the Quran and has been used throughout history, it has been misused and exploited by political and religious organizations. It is therefore deeply concerning that it is presented without discussion to students who are given no reason to question its prevailing sociocultural meaning. As one teacher observed, "the training we received … lacked [a] participatory or critical approach and the teachers [have] been told to implement the curricula as it is." The textbooks also praise heroes in ways that may instigate violence or encourage pro-violence values. The media, many teachers and parents, as well as textbooks certainly endorse the cultural convention that the *peshmergah*— of whom there are more than 150,000 in IK, many connected to school-age students—deserve great respect.

The textbooks present, with little discussion or critical perspective, many other discriminatory and archaic concepts that were prevalent in the Islamic era and in Kurdish history. For example, crusaders are defined simply as "people who came from Europe and attacked Muslims and had Christian symbols on their clothes." This context-free binarized description is typical in the way it uncritically presents a narrow version of the truth, highly aligned with conventional accepted views in contemporary IK.

IK's teachers generally deliver history curricula without adding critical perspective. Our interviewees explained to us that they only "teach what is in the textbooks because otherwise students will complain and the teachers would have to include these definitions in the exams." In IK's HEC, key concepts such as war, conflict, liberation, invasion, conquest, Jihad battles, and other terms, are used in ways that reinforce the dominant social group's views. Some of the teachers we interviewed, however, voiced criticism over this approach and suggested that "the teachers know better what students need to know; hence, they should be given more freedom."

Muslim leaders have declared that there is a need to end discrimination and racism among Muslims, and this view is promoted in HE textbooks. Muslim leaders can play constructive roles in sharing peaceful messages with the different ethnic and religious groups in IK, but their ideas need to be explained clearly and linked to current contexts if they are to be effective. At the present time, IK's HE textbooks address non-discrimination weakly and focus on it only as a problem among Muslims, rather than between Muslims and non-Muslims.

When IK's HEC suggest that inequality existed in the past and that preferential treatment for Muslims over non-Muslims was legitimized, these facts are delivered without critical commentary or consideration of their contemporary relevance to IK's status as a multiethnic and religious society. The textbooks describe methods that Islamic-era Muslim leaders used to differentiate between Muslims and non-Muslims after the Prophet's death. For example, the seventh-year textbook explains that in the Abbassi State era (656 CE) there were attempts to end discrimination between Arab Muslims and non-Arab Muslims, and the fifth-year textbook states that non-Muslims who lived within the borders of Islamic State had to pay *Jizya* (Tax) for being non-Muslims.

The absence of critical analysis in relation to past discrimination is of particular concern in IK because, although there is a Muslim majority, Christian, Yezidi, Sabai, Buhai, Shabak, and other religious groups also exist. Even segregated Christian and Yezidi schools use IK's standard textbooks, and the negative representation of groups who live alongside each other is liable to foster resentment and hierarchized divisions between Muslims and non-Muslims based on religious affiliation rather than citizenship. The HE textbooks clearly differentiate between Muslims and non-Muslims and marginalize other ethnic religious groups. Jews are represented as untrustworthy, while Christianity and Zaradashti are presented as religions undeserving of worship. Claims that "the Prophet Mohammed came to spread the message of Islam to all people" and that he was a "messenger to all mankind" help to delegitimize and undermine non-dominant ethnic and religious groups.

When the textbooks deal with the history of Kurdistan, they overlook non-Muslim groups. The seventh-year textbook refers to various ancient societies within Kurdistan but ignores the Yezidis. Ministry of Education officials told us that this was because Yezidis are considered to be Kurdish, but Yezidi teachers countered that "the ME is lacking in fairness and inclusiveness." One head teacher explained that, "despite the fact we have complained many times to the ME about not having a Yezidi committee to represent us like the Christians and Turkmen have, they did not reply to us—we feel marginalized."

The exclusion of non-Muslim religious and ethnic groups from HE curricula implies that they are insignificant and so strengthens prejudices and stereotypes against them. The HEC should at least highlight similarities between the peace values that religions share in order to encourage harmony and cooperation. Instead, the explicit and implicit content of IK's history textbooks suggest the superiority of Islam and imply the inferior spiritual status of other religions.

While IK's HEC mainly focus on teaching war values, they do discuss the role and responsibilities of the state in providing services to and protection for citizens. One textbook asserts that the state should foster "economic development and the provision of social services," and while equality is only mentioned once, there are references to tranquility, friendship, stabilization, security, and brotherhood. Concepts such as forgiveness and reconciliation, and the peaceful values associated with different interpretations of Islam, however, are not recognized.

The different traditional legal schools of thought in Sunni Sharia go undiscussed, and women's roles are rarely addressed in the HE textbooks, which reflect the patriarchal nature of IK society, even though there have been many women leaders in Kurdish and Iraqi history. The school system could play a critical role in fostering gender equality by remedying this imbalance. Textbook exercises could also, theoretically, encourage students to participate in producing information in the classroom and relate it to their own social and political contexts; however, at the present time, such exercises take the form of rote-style recall and repeat questions, which make up 54 out of 55 questions in the fifth-year book alone.

In general, the HEC curriculum teaches one approach to understanding reality: the Kurds are always right, while the Iraqi government and the international community are wrong; Muslims are right and disbelievers are wrong, and all negative characteristics are attributed to the other. One teacher commented approvingly that "the Ministry of Education is right to give one narrative as it wants to unite people, make them agree on one statement; for us to have different opinions we need another fifty years of self-rule and independence."

The present HE curricula inhibit exploration of other possible narratives. Information is presented as unequivocally true, and students are not directed to sources that might provide alternative perspectives. This binarized approach to right or wrong and legitimate or illegitimate forms of knowledge works to restrict students' creativity and critical thinking and increase their dependency on teachers and other authority figures. While learners often take the blame for their passivity and their ignorance of nuanced narratives, the curriculum, its contents, processes, and delivery, clearly help to limit their knowledge and work to normalize and fuel cycles of violence.

In IK, the dominant group is clearly using HEC to stabilize and legitimize its authority. IK's HE textbooks ostensibly provide a straightforward description of events in history, and many students and teachers in IK schools understand them as neutral: one teacher explained that "HE is about knowing facts, story events, dates, numbers." Others appreciate, however, that when students are not skillful enough to challenge authoritative knowledge and seek out diverse narratives, HEC texts contribute to the state's hegemony by offering an accepted and common interpretation of its character and narrative that becomes embedded and normalized in social consciousness.

To be effective in terms of PE values and education for peace, HEC must be enquiry-based and open to variations, different interpretations, and critical debate; they must also begin a process of de-victimization and encourage a more heterogeneous collective narrative to emerge. Children learn a huge amount about history from their communities and families as well as from the media and school curricula. Nevertheless, the failure to provide students with a balanced perspective on the violence prevalent in IK's society helps dominant norms to go unchallenged and embeds in young people's minds an almost uncontestable single narrative about their shared past, present, and future.

RECOMMENDED READINGS

Aziz, Mahir A. 2011. *Ethno-Nationalism and National Identity in Iraqi Kurdistan*. London: I. B. Tauris.

Bekerman, Zvi, and Michalinos Zembylas. 2012. *Teaching Contested Narratives: Identity, Memory and Reconciliation in Peace Education and Beyond*. Cambridge: Cambridge University Press.

Cremin, Hilary. 2016. "Peace Education Research in the Twenty-First Century: Three Concepts Facing Crisis or Opportunity?" *Journal of Peace Education* 13 (1):1–17.

Löfgren, Hors. 1995. *Peace Education and Human Development*. Malmo: Malmo School of Education.

Salomon, Gavriel, and Baruch Nevo, eds. 2002. *Peace Education: The Concept, Principles and Practices Around the World*. Hillsdale, NJ: Lawrence Erlbaum.

Transrational Peacebuilding Education to Reduce Epistemic Violence

HILARY CREMIN, JOSEFINA ECHAVARRÍA AND KEVIN KESTER

We believe there are three crises facing peacebuilding education today. The first is the nationalism present in many peace education programs. The second is the continuing cultural imposition of Western ideology and colonialism through peace education efforts. The third is the dominant reliance on rational forms of learning often inconsistent with the transformative and inclusive purposes of peace education. At the core of these three crises is a question about the role of the peace scholar in either disrupting or perpetuating these norms. What follows outlines the tenets of these problems, offers some reflections on research that illustrate the challenges in practice, and finally, presents some pedagogic responses for teaching peace (and challenging war) in the twenty-first century that we believe could overcome some of these challenges for peacebuilding education.

Yet before we begin, we offer a short synopsis of our own positions within peacebuilding education. We do this in recognition that this essay has been co-written by three authors, in a polyphonic way, bringing our diverse but resonant voices together. While a detailed presentation of our perspectives cannot be included here for reasons of space, it is important to highlight how we are positioned in relation to peacebuilding education. Our work intersects as we try to come to terms with issues of structural and cultural violence in education and society, and to de-nationalize and de-colonize peacebuilding education through our efforts toward transnational, transrational, and transformational peacebuilding. Hilary hopes that her work offers alternative imaginaries for peace education, drawing on the global East and South, and placing embodiment, affect, care, eco-systemic thinking, and spirituality at the heart of the educational enterprise. Josefina's emphasis is on embracing the conflictual and relational character of peace(building) that is central to the facilitation of safe spaces where learners can try out new ways of relating to others and themselves. Kevin's work is skeptical of ethnocentric and psycho-social approaches to peacebuilding that overlook or de-emphasize the social dimensions. He promotes a transnational and cosmopolitan approach. Together, we remain hopeful that peacebuilding education can offer transformative possibilities for the cultivation of a more humane and just world.

Peacebuilding education tends to function at the level of the state, with *pax romana*—the cessation in hostilities—conceived as the uneasy peace that can exist between nations. With the nation-state taking center stage as the focus of analysis in political and educational discourse, the complexity of intra-state and ethnic conflict is often lost, not to mention interpersonal or intrapersonal conflict. The universal assumptions that are associated with state-building (for example, beliefs in the permanence and righteousness of the state, the equilibrium of liberal economics, and emancipatory possibilities of representative democracy as pedagogic pathways to peace) also serve to close down diverse understandings of what it is to live in a globalized world. More than this, as Ilan Gur Ze-ev, Zvi, Bekerman, and Michalinos Zembylas point out, peacebuilding education has often been complicit in nation-building, and in the perpetuation of state-based values and norms. This has the potential to bring about the opposite of what peacebuilding aspires toward. Thus, this first arena of concern operates at the level of an educational discourse that is essentialist toward states as the ultimate harbingers of peace.

The educational discourse of states as harbingers of peace focuses on learning about universal human rights, lobbying of the state through civil society, and the promotion of transitional justice mechanisms. In this approach, mediation and negotiation training exercises typically aim to educate citizens to engage the state (rather than communities) in an effort toward social pressure to transform the state. The state remains the focus. It is incumbent on peace educators, then, to find ways to respond positively to threats of war and violence by engaging both the state and local communities—or what Oliver Richmond might call the hybrid approach. It is therefore important for educational peacebuilders to work to build sustainable peace through the kinds of community peacebuilding processes advocated by scholars such as John Paul Lederach and Ivan Illich. A curricular implication of this is the import for a both/and teaching approach (that is, teaching about the state, but also so much more). This links to the second crisis.

Second, the dominance of Western thinking in peacebuilding education is evident through a comprehensive review of its literature. Such literature typically draws on Western notions of peace (such as the state) that ignore (or exoticize and commercialize) concepts of peace that come from the global South and East. For example, the majority of institutions and scholars named in peace literature tend to be North American,

British, or Western European. The problem here is that Western knowledge becomes normalized in heterogeneous contexts, with the curricular implication being the necessary development of decolonial educational approaches that critique and seek to transform the assumed norms of peacebuilding education. The promotion of alternative educational pedagogies, such as South–South simulations, historical recontextualization, and embodied learning, could be actions taken to expand the field beyond its colonial limitations. This leads into the third crisis.

The third crisis concerns the teaching of peace through critical democratic pedagogy. While critical pedagogy is important to raise students' awareness of issues of conflict in society, it should nonetheless be noted that such pedagogy emerges from the Enlightenment legacy of rationalism. Hence, some forms of critical democratic pedagogy in peacebuilding education are overly cognate, and overlook the role of emotions and affect in learning. For example, critical pedagogy advantages direct forms of communication based in rationality and active and analytic forms of thinking, while it disadvantages indirect supposedly nonrational approaches and embodied ways of being. The implication of this is that space for alternative epistemologies and peacebuilding practices must be provided to invite diverse responses. Then, greater attention to the body and emotion and experiences of trauma are needed to transcend the field's rational limitations based in critical theory/pedagogy.

We offer here some brief reflections on research into United Nations (UN) higher education. Many are not aware that the UN operates two universities. For over 40 years the UN, via these universities, has conducted research and taught peace to postgraduate students from around the world. Yet very little research has examined the curriculum, teaching, and effect of the UN higher education institutions on students and communities. To fill this void, in critical research elsewhere, one of the authors (Kevin Kester) has empirically shown how the teaching at one UN case institution (which will remain anonymous) is implicated in the philosophical and pedagogical critiques we outlined above. This brief section then will illustrate those critiques in practice at the university of the UN. We begin first with nationalism. It should be borne in mind throughout that, although we are focusing on the critiques here, there still remains much positive work in the institution.

Nationalism at the university is manifest in two ways. It is initially realized through the emphasis on cultural representation in the institution with students coming from over 60 different countries. Frequently in classes, according to the students and faculty interviewed, students were expected to speak on behalf of their home cultures/states. Many students expressed their appreciation of the cultural diversity in the university, but also felt that there is a risk of reinforcing stereotypes in this approach to multicultural representational teaching. As well, nationalism is present via the emphasis in the curriculum on the analysis of state-level conflicts and state-based simulations. For example, one professor in Kester's study claimed, "When many people think of peacebuilding they focus too much on state-level negotiation, mediation, et cetera, [they] want to be the guys at Camp David."

In itself nationalism and the state-orientation is not necessarily problematic unless it operates at an unknowing or taken-for-granted level. It is important for peace scholars to interrogate the operations and violences embedded within national and cultural fronts that are often normalized. This argument is then entangled with colonialism, as a critical reading of nationalism and culture would contest that not all states and societies are perceived equally in the current global order. Kester furthermore witnessed this in the dominance of the Western influence on curriculum. This leads to the second crisis point.

S econd, as Kester has shown in *Teaching in Higher Education*, colonial Western-centricity dominates the teaching and learning at these institutions. This materializes in three ways: first, through the Western background and ethnicity of the scholars who teach in the university; second, through the curriculum that lecturers teach; and, third, through the academic pedigree of the scholars, including those from the Global South. Although the majority of lecturers (21/25) in the institution were Western, they were also ethnically diverse, which raises interesting questions concerning the scholars' role in the reproduction of Western-centricity and privilege in the university. For example, minority Northern scholars, and Latin American and Asian lecturers alike, largely emphasized a normative Western liberal peacebuilding model (with some exceptions). Furthermore, from the point of view of the taught curriculum, it was noticeable that among the commonly assigned scholars in syllabi the most frequently assigned were Western, White men in particular. Because the most commonly assigned scholars were thus, this suggests a degree of Western normativity in the institution. This is especially problematic given the multicultural demographic of the student body. Students agreed.

In regard to the academic background of the scholars, all of the lecturers except two were educated in Western institutions, and one of these two scholars later spent an impressive part of her career lecturing in a Western university. Hence, as Kester has explained, only one of the UN academics had never worked or studied in a Western institution. The ethnicity of scholars, curricular content, and learned backgrounds of study participants then exhibits a tilt toward Western normativity in the university. This brings us to our third crisis on pedagogy.

Third, equally dominant in the classes Kester observed, with some notable exceptions, was the faith attributed to critical discourse and dialogue as the primary modality of rational peace teaching. This occurred in at least two ways. First, the pedagogy employed was primarily lectures and dialogical seminars with a focus on analytical thinking and critique. Second, there was an assumption that proper critical classroom teaching could lead to democratic benefits for society more widely via increased civic participation. These premises were raised through extensive classroom observations and post-observation interviews with faculty and students. Perhaps surprisingly, in the observations, those lecturers who stood and lectured (teaching to the students' heads) were regarded by students as more knowledgeable for peacebuilding education (as expressed by students in interviews), while those lecturers who sat (teaching to the students' bodies) were regarded as less experienced. In this way, the assumed correlation between knowledge and mind-centric pedagogies undergirded a peacebuilding education that was grounded in rationality and mind-orientedness, which may again place the practice within a Western frame of reference.

I n the interviews, faculty members indicated their belief in participatory democratic classroom learning as contributing toward global democracy. This sentiment is well encapsulated in other literature. Betty Reardon and Alicia Cabezudo, for example, argue, "Education for global citizenship in a culture of peace requires a pedagogy of democratic engagement. Active and participatory engagement of students in the learning process ... is the most relevant and effective pedagogy to prepare students for active participation in ... global civil society." It is hard to argue against this, but we feel that, while critical democratic pedagogy is important to challenge structural violence and to envision alternative social arrangements, it still remains somewhat limited in its analytic, rational, and psycho-social approach. Instead, we now call for a transrational pedagogy that gives attention to the emotional, embodied, and metaphysical aspects of peace learning. We equally feel that transnational education is an appropriate response to the limits of nationalism in peacebuilding education, and that transformational peacebuilding education can go beyond the limits of colonialism. There is not space to go into these areas in this short essay, so we turn now to focus on transrational pedagogy as the core of this essay.

Peacebuilding educational initiatives have tried to tackle the criticisms of nationalism, colonialism, and rationalism in myriad ways. Unlike, however, many modern traditions of peacebuilding education in their idealist, realist, or critical variations, we find transrational peace education to be a promising example of an alternative approach. This approach first raises a critique of a purely rational educational idea of peace, as we have above, and from there derives a series of embodied pedagogies that address the human being in all her faculties, not just the mental and psychological dimensions. For example, from a philosophical point of view, Wolfgang Dietrich argues that it is not only rationality that is relevant for our comprehension of peace. As human beings we are rational, yet also so much more, so that peace has embodied, emotional, and spiritual dimensions, as well as mental ones. Transrationality is thus an understanding that includes rationality and critical discernment, but is also open to systemic and transpersonal approaches.

If peace is understood transrationally, the pedagogy to "teach" peace studies then needs to reflect a holistic perspective in which several dimensions of the self are mobilized and attuned for learning peace. Following Dietrich's categorizations, and those further developed by the authors, these are breath, voice, and movement-oriented methods. These methods can be translated into pedagogical tools that seek to address that which is tangible, measurable, and manifest (as in critical democratic pedagogy) but they do not stop there. These pedagogies reach much deeper layers of being. In our work in Innsbruck, Austria; Cambridge, UK; and Daegu, Korea, the integration and differentiation of rationality into the curriculum takes the form of classical seminars and lectures, as well as simulations during excursions and workshops, and opportunities for learners to engage with transformative embodied pedagogies like Theatre for Living, Systemic Constellations, Qi Gong, and Holotropic Breathwork.

The logical consequence of a transrational peace approach, as briefly defined above, is that relations between learners and facilitators, as well as among learners, are based on "elicitive" values. As John Paul Lederach has coined it, "elicitive" invites conflict analysts and mediators to discover the knowledge, experiences, and communication styles that are already present in the conflictive settings in order to catalyze their potential for peaceful conflict transformation. The values that result from an elicitive approach underpin deeply participatory learning: learners are encouraged to discover peace and conflict in themselves—not only outside the classroom in conflict situations removed from their personal lives. Their knowledge and experiences are valid epistemologies, their voices are heard and recognized, and the didactics allow new possibilities for testing their own modalities for conflict transformation.

In Lederach's model, the trainer, and (in the peacebuilding education model) the facilitator of learning, is seen as another element in the system. The facilitator seeks to catalyze the existing knowledge, not just by bringing in knowledge from other contexts, but by empowering learners through awareness of themselves, others, and the environment. The methodologies arising from the transrational educational approach additionally require that the students' bodies, as well as the bodies of faculty and staff, are diverse. This diversity includes the individuals' identity backgrounds, and importantly, the content and sources of the educational material. This combination of a philosophical approach to peace, and the pedagogic and curricular enactment of it through various means, such as breathwork, meditation, Qi Gong, artistic expression, and cooperative learning, allows for epistemological pluralism. It goes hand-in-hand with the corresponding curricula, staff and student experiences, and diverse pedagogies that form a coherent framework for peacebuilding education that might offer possible windows into the transrational self. The transrational approach is one example among many other positive developments that the field of peacebuilding education is seeing proliferate around the world, each of which are seeking to satisfy the needs of learning communities to embrace the power of plural peaces.

In conclusion, the field of peacebuilding education has tended to focus on national, colonial, and rational discourses, such as Western conceptions of the state, state-oriented protections of human rights, and critical democratic pedagogy. It has been overly preoccupied with human rights frameworks and active citizenship, at the expense of other ways of understanding peace and harmony. In this, peacebuilding education has promoted disinterested rationalities of peace realized through attending to international normative standards. Our research illustrates the presence of nationalism, rationalism, and colonialism in peacebuilding education today, and as such, our higher education teaching practices lean toward the elicitive, the embodied, and the metaphysical, as well as the rational. We suggest that the limits and possibilities for a transrational peacebuilding education must be interrogated in and through education in order to more fully cultivate an inclusive and transformative peacebuilding education for the twenty-first century.

RECOMMENDED READINGS

Bekerman, Zvi, and Michalinos Zembylas. 2012. *Teaching Contested Narratives: Identity, Memory and Reconciliation in Peace Education and Beyond.* Cambridge, UK: Cambridge University Press.

Connell, Raewyn. 2007. *Southern Theory: The Global Dynamics of Knowledge in Social Science.* Sydney, Australia: Allen & Unwin.

Cremin, Hilary, and Terence Bevington. 2017. *Positive Peace in Schools: Tackling Conflict and Creating a Culture of Peace in the Classroom*. London, UK: Routledge

Dietrich, Wolfgang. 2012. *Interpretations of Peace in History and Culture*. London, UK: Palgrave Macmillan.

Echavarria, Josefina. 2014. "Elicitive Conflict Mapping: A Practical Tool for Peace Work." *Journal of Conflictology* 5 (2):58–71.

Echavarría, Josefina, Daniela Ingruber, and Norbert Koppensteiner (Eds.). 2018. *Transrational Resonances: Echoes to the Many Peaces*. London, UK: Palgrave Macmillan.

Gur Ze-Ev, Ilan. 2010. *Diasporic Philosophy and Counter-Education*. Rotterdam. The Netherlands: Sense Publishers.

Kester, Kevin. 2017. "The Case of Educational Peacebuilding Inside the United Nations Universities: A Review and Critique." *Journal of Transformative Education* 15 (1):59–78.

Kester, Kevin. 2018. "Reproducing Peace? A CRT Analysis of Whiteness in the Curriculum and Teaching at a University of the UN." *Teaching in Higher Education* 23:1.

Lederach, John Paul. 1995. *Preparing for Peace: Conflict Transformation Across Cultures*. Syracuse, NY: Syracuse University.

Reardon, Betty, and Alicia Cabezudo. 2002. *Learning to Abolish War*. New York, NY: Hague Appeal for Peace.

de Sousa Santos, Boaventura. 2007. *Epistemologies of the South: Justice Against Epistemicide*. London, UK: Paradigm.

Teaching Tangible Peace

PATRICK T. HILLER

War is rarely questioned and is deeply engrained in the U.S. educational system as a natural and necessary act by a good entity—usually the United States—fighting evil. War is the sometimes tragic, sometimes heroic, but almost always necessary part of our history. Peace is wishful thinking. History is commonly presented as a succession of wars interspersed with notable events that one might consider anomalies. War is the domain for studies and public intellectual expertise. Peace is left to the hopelessly naïve. This does not have to be the case.

Hundreds of undergraduate and graduate programs in peace and conflict studies exist around the world. Peace Studies, with all the variations of the exact course titles examine issues of war and peace. Graduate students worldwide focus on the subject matter and advance their education in peace and conflict studies. Undergraduate students, in my experience, come in with a very different mentality. I have taught almost 25 classes of undergraduate introductory courses in peace and conflict studies. Most students end up in the course to fulfill cluster requirements and demonstrate at least some curiosity about the studies of conflict, war, and peace. The most common theme of the more than 700 students in those courses was their unawareness of peace and conflict studies as a field with theories and practices to transform conflicts without violence. They also felt encouraged to use the acquired knowledge in their own lives and ready and willing to take more courses in the field. These experiences are the context of my thoughts on teaching about peace and war.

Teaching about war and peace should contain two main, interconnected elements. First, I make a case for using a war system and peace system perspective when teaching peace studies. Second, educators should situate their teaching within the theoretical field of peace and conflict studies, which is accompanied by an increasingly professional field of practice. I explain how the war system and the peace system can be examined as competing practical and ideological constructs. I discuss key components of both systems. Then I demonstrate how students can be engaged in a methodological inquiry on war and peace systems through structured conflict analysis and assignments that demonstrate the reality of peace systems in our everyday lives. I then show how the more structured inquiry and understanding of war and peace issues enhances career possibilities, creates stronger peace advocacy, and ultimately can contribute to structural transformation of a militarized society toward a society built on cultures of peace. I conclude by tasking those of us who self-identify as peace educators to embrace and improve the already solid field of peace and conflict studies, rather than letting peace and peace studies remain a pollyannish construct not to be taken seriously compared to traditional disciplines and "hard" sciences.

Wars are commonly based on a set of beliefs about conflict that make them inevitable, natural, and fought with good intentions by good versus evil. Wars are believed to break out as crises beyond our control. Students carry these social myths about war into the classroom. Therefore, it is important to not only de-construct some of the factually wrong myths about war being natural, war having always been there, war being beneficial or war being necessary, but also examine how a war system has locked beliefs into our society upholding those myths. This means we need to critically examine militarism in all its manifestations. Some components of the war system in the United States are the military organization itself, the governmental security and intelligence organizations, the glorification of war in the media and at sports events, the weapons manufacturers, and the connection to the government and elections and recruitment techniques in the school systems.

An examination of the war system broadens the understanding of the costs of war. The number of U.S. soldiers killed is the most common public reference point to measure the costs of war. Of course, depending on the source, foreign combatants and civilians killed are not left unmentioned. The costs and implications of a war system, however, reach far beyond the obvious ones. For example, one can include discussions about U.S. poverty and racism and the notion of poverty draft, referring to the disproportionate presence of men and women of color and/or from a lower socioeconomic background in the military. One can also connect to a wide range of environmental concerns by looking at military fossil fuel consumption, the contamination of soil through weapons production and use, the causation of birth defects and cancer, or the destruction of wildlife habitat. Working with students on identifying war system variables helps shed light on how a shift from war to peace requires us to think beyond simplistic causal relationships of specific wars that "broke out," and instead recognize that the war system itself needs to be challenged and replaced.

Peace systems concepts are attractive in that they give the often-overused concept of peace a concrete meaning and pathways toward achieving it. Starting in the 1940s, scholars have used the peace systems concept on few occasions. What compelled me to fully adopt a peace systems perspective in my teaching was historian and peace educator Kent Shifferd's recognition of a Global Peace System based on 28 revolutionary historic global trends that began in the early nineteenth century. I categorized the trends into three main categories of global collaboration, constructive conflict transformation, and social change. Specific trends include the emergence of international institutions to prevent war, the evolution of nonviolence as a form of struggle, the rise of global civil society, the multiple rights movements, and many more.

Peace and conflict studies and professionally applied peacebuilding techniques take the "soft" out of peace. For a peace system to be considered a counterforce to the war system it needs to be disconnected from a narrative depicting it as weak and naïve when compared to a war system. Students usually are not aware of the field of peace and conflict studies with hundreds of university programs worldwide; textbooks, conferences, and associations like the International Peace Research Association and its regional affiliates; and peace research institutions like the Stockholm International Peace Research Institute or the Peace Research Institute Oslo. While interdisciplinary in nature, Elise Boulding, Johan Galtung, and the many other founding mothers and fathers of our field have developed a field unique in its objective of examining the causes of war and the conditions for peace with the normative aim of nonviolent conflict transformation. Galtung envisioned theories guiding peace workers to contribute to positive peace—peace with justice. The founders also envisioned bridging the gap between the moral outlook of the peace movement and foreign policy pragmatism.

In my own research with long-time nonviolent peace movement activists in the United States, I have found that peace activists clearly understood the war system and culture of militarism. In sharing their life stories, activists talked about their experiences related to the Civil Rights Movement, the Anti–Vietnam War Movement, conscientious objection, the opposition to nuclear power and weapons, the Latin/Central America Solidarity Movement, the ongoing movements opposing the wars in Iraq and Afghanistan, and the Middle East Conflict in general, to name just a few. While several movements and actions were successful, the peace movement is still sidelined from the mainstream narrative for its perceived naivety. Issues of national security and war and peace are best left to the "experts." The good news is: peace and conflict studies is producing the experts and professionalizing peace. Students tend to be unaware of what I call an increasingly professionalized field of peacebuilding, most visible in the United States through the Alliance for Peacebuilding and its more than 100 organizational members or the Peace and Security Funders Group and its approximately 70 members. Creating the awareness of the reality of these peace networks lays the groundwork for recognizing the peace system as real, albeit not as dominating as the war system.

Merely talking about the war and peace system in classes is not enough. Students need to be engaged methodologically to activate their imagination and develop the capacity to connect the dots of the war and peace system. First, any approach toward understanding war and peace issues requires conflict analysis. That is the structured inquiry into the causes and potential trajectory of a conflict that seeks to identify opportunities managing, transforming, and resolving it nonviolently. Conflict analysis provides a complete picture of a conflict, which, combined with the war and peace systems concepts, allows us to identify the many dynamics at play rather than falling back to overly simplistic explanations for wars and other large-scale violent conflict. When studying past wars, we understand no war has ever been traced back to a single cause and the constantly reinforced good versus evil narrative. Conflict analysis will often reveal political, ethnic, religious, or resource conflicts within one single context. Moreover, the analysis will reveal that many of the dynamics at play are part of the war system that permeates U.S. society and its core institutions.

A second teaching tool is the Global Peace System timeline. I have developed this tool to visualize the systemic nature and growth of the Global Peace System over time in a multidimensional, high-resolution graphic that can be used online and in print. The vertical dimension contains the main categories of "Social Change," "Conflict Transformation," and "Global Collaboration." Three colors allow the user to distinguish between the categories. Within the three main categories, the 28 trends constituting the Global Peace System are listed, representing the vertical axis of the timeline. Up to five historical events from the horizontal axis are directly attributed to the respective trend and connected to the trend through a very thin line. By using this kind of illustration, the rich historical data that usually would fill many written pages is presented in a high resolution printed or screen form on one page. The overall visual impression is an accumulation of historical peace trends that are intertwined and become stronger over time. The inspiration for this approach was primarily the work of data visualization specialist Edward R. Tufte. Some of the major elements of Tufte's practical philosophy are: display information, provide large amounts of information in a coherent manner, reveal information at different levels of detail, encourage the eye to compare different pieces of information, go from a general perspective to details and develop a sense of curiosity.

Third, I create assignments for students to identify the components of the war and peace system through the examination of credible current news, commentary, reports, and other sources. For example, when discussing the impact of corporations or institutions on global warfare and violence, students need to find examples and connect the institutions' official narratives and information to what a war systems analysis might reveal. Another example to show the increasingly maturing peace system focuses on nonviolent campaigns. Nonviolent action is most readily associated with the names of Mahatma Gandhi, Martin Luther King Jr., and Nelson Mandela, three personalities who dedicated their lives toward achieving social change by nonviolent ways. Given what is happening in the world today, nonviolent action is one of the most important subjects to highlight when teaching about war and peace. In class, students are required to research a current campaign of nonviolent action related to the peace studies course. Evaluating the submissions is by far the most rewarding grading of all courses I have taught. In every class about 30 students come up with just as many examples of nonviolent action that they can situate within the trends of the Global Peace System. The exercise helps to clear up misperceptions about nonviolent action: First, nonviolent action has nothing to do with passivity; second, it is less spontaneous than it is strategic; third, people who use nonviolent action do not have to be pacifists or saints; and fourth, nonviolent action has been/is far more frequent and widespread than supposed.

When educating on war and peace, the task at hand is clear. The war system needs to be examined thoroughly and recognized as destructive and dominant. The peace system needs to be examined as real and growing based on global trends and increasingly professionalized peace practices. Why does this matter? Students who enroll in peace studies courses, even at an undergraduate level and outside of their major and minors demonstrate willingness to at least be confronted with the issues. The perspectives as laid out in this essay will allow for stronger peace advocacy, since the arguments are based on analysis and evidence, not wishful thinking.

Moreover, a peace systems perspective broadens students' horizons for possible careers in the field. In a talk on careers in strategic peacebuilding, George Lopez from Notre Dame's Kroc Institute for International Peace Studies outlined a total of 78 different possible careers in areas such as restorative justice, nonviolent social change, government, dialogue and conflict resolution, or dealing with transnational threats. The potential effect on students is obvious. They now can imagine themselves concretely in peacebuilding careers without being labeled as naïve students merely satisfying their intellectual curiosity in university education. In the long term, as peace educators adopting the peace systems perspective we can help guide more students into such careers and equip them to challenge the war system with tools from our field to contribute to structural transformation toward a peace system.

As educators in a discipline that is young and not always given the recognition it deserves in academia, we need to be open to scrutiny and rigorous in our analysis. Since we do not only theorize on war and peace issues in a social vacuum, we need to navigate the normative goal for peace with the empirical and analytical rigor demanded from scholarly inquiry. We need to situate our courses, but also certificates, minors, and majors in the field of peace and conflict studies. We must not fall into the trap of considering everything that feels good to be part of peace studies. The founding mothers and fathers of our field deserve that we build on their pioneering work and ensure that our field is recognized, solid, and contributes to a more just and peaceful world.

The concept of the Global Peace System can help us advance these goals in the classroom. The trends are observed from a global perspective. At the same time, all trends have regional, local, and even personal implications. Examining the reality of global trends based on real-life examples is an active creation of an alternative history and present where the dominant societal narrative still considers war inevitable. Students' initial "I had no idea" can be the starting point for their informed path toward working for peace and justice and state with confidence that there are better and more effective alternatives to war and violence.

RECOMMENDED READINGS

Pilisuk, Marc, and Jennifer A. Rountree. 2015. *The Hidden Structure of Violence: Who Benefits from Global Violence and War*. New York, NY: New York University Press.

Shifferd, Kent D. 2011. *From War to Peace: A Guide to the Next Hundred Years*. Jefferson, IA: McFarland.

Teaching the United Nations, Gender, and Critical Pedagogy

GEORGINA HOLMES

Chair of the Committee on Teaching about the United Nations, Anne-Marie Carlson, once argued in *UN Chronicle* that, "unless students come to know and appreciate the mandate and role of the United Nations (UN) in helping their world become safer and more humane, far too many of mankind's failures will simply be repeated." It is now fairly common practice in British universities for Politics and International Relations departments to offer undergraduate modules that examine the UN's efforts to respond to international security challenges. Investigating complex, multilevel relations of power that structure and operate through the international security institution, such modules aim to teach students about inequalities and social justice. Yet, do the critical pedagogic approaches adopted by teachers fully succeed in deconstructing the UN's institutionalized power relations? Applying an intersectional feminist lens to the analysis of curriculum design, I examine how two undergraduate modules taught at British universities between 2013 and 2016 are structured according to a repressive 'neo-liberal gender logic', and consider the implications this has for how gendered war and peace are conceptualized; and how male and female students are socialized as future employees of institutions. I then reflect on the pedagogic practices I have adopted in partnership with students to challenge this repressive logic.

F eminist scholars have long argued that feminist theory and pedagogy has been pushed to the margins of international relations degree courses. In the early 1990s, Christine Sylvester and others levied criticism that feminist theoretical paradigms were absent in undergraduate teaching because they did not fit, as Christina Rowley and Laura Shepherd have described, "the dominant rationalist orthodoxy" of the discipline. This rationalist orthodoxy, drawn from Realist and Liberalist paradigms that produce abstract, systemic-level analyses, determined how international security institutions were conceptualized through the pedagogic encounter. With the opening up of the discipline and the growing prominence of

Critical theory, the old rationalist orthodoxy was required to make way for an expanding and diverse range of paradigms that include less- and non-mainstream theories. Politics and International Relations (IR) departments in British universities have veered toward using "plural pedagogy" and adopting a multiparadigm approach to the study of international relations, as John Craig observes.

In spite of continued resistance, the Critical turn in IR and the persistence of feminist scholars has meant that feminist IR theory is now part of the mainstream curricula of most British B.A. IR degree courses. Aside from specialist "gender modules," the most pronounced discursive space wherein feminist paradigms are incorporated are core IR theory modules that all students are expected to take. Usually taught in year one or year two of the three-year degree course, each week of these modules broaches a different theory and observes the evolution of IR theorizing—moving from teaching the old rationalist orthodoxy in the first semester to teaching post-positivist theories in the second semester, which is often dedicated entirely to the Critical School.

For Rowley and Shepherd, "the week on gender," much like the "chapter on gender" in IR theory textbooks demonstrates little progress toward transforming male-centric engagements with IR, beyond adopting the "add women and stir" approach to explaining women's experiences and international security. Proponents of pluralist pedagogy and critical pedagogy may dispute this claim, arguing that these teaching praxes actually prevent the ghettoization of non-mainstream theories and methodologies. The rationale here is that iterative learning combined with critical pedagogy, with its focus on exposing inequalities, challenge dominant and disciplining knowledge claims, facilitate the transformation of existing power relations in society, and contribute to institutionalizing social justice.

Isreali Philosopher Ilan Gur-Ze'ev once wrote that critical pedagogy should be a "counter-education" to "hegemonic-education" and a mechanism through which to resist "violent practices of normalization, control and reproduction practices in a system that uses human beings as agents and victims." Key to this, according to the liberatory pedagogy of Paulo Freire, is dialogue between students and teachers, wherein the teaching and learning environment enables "equal, open and critical intersubjectivity between students and their world ... and in the space in which they are located, as an alternative to power relations within the school and the apparatuses and hierarchies that constitute them."

With this in mind, it is important to assess how feminist paradigms and gender issues are integrated into individual modules in the context of the overarching structure and learning objectives of the undergraduate degree course, since students will bring to the classroom knowledge of a plurality of theoretical paradigms, as well as personal perspectives.

In *UN Chronicle*, Carlson advocated for critical pedagogy as the most appropriate approach when teaching about the UN, contending that "education efforts should not just highlight [the UN's] successes but also acknowledge the limitations and weaknesses that affect [the security institution's] performance." Six imperatives should be factored into the curriculum design of educational courses. Top of her list was the significance of acknowledging the UN's "major role in decolonisation and the emergence of some 80 new sovereign states"; "the huge disparity between the haves and have-nots"; and the work of the UN's specialized agencies such as the World Food Programme and United Nations Development Programme.

Carlson also expected students to comprehend the machinations of the institution's principal organs, including the Security Council, the Secretariat, the General Assembly, and the Economic and Social Council. Without this knowledge—and without developing critical perspectives—students (Carlson's "younger generation") would be less likely to use "their creativity and resourcefulness" to solve the global issues the UN seeks to address. While not necessarily destined to work in governments or the UN, this generation would likely become employers and leaders of "business, service industries, technologies, agriculture and other essential vocations." Students should develop vested political interests in the UN's external program of work but should accept the UN's institutional ways of working.

The curriculum design of the two long-standing modules, taught in British universities between 2013 and 2016 and selected as case studies for this essay, succeed in delivering on Carlson's six imperatives. Both are optional modules available to Politics and IR students, as well as to students studying Law, Economics, and History. Case Study A is offered to second-year students while Case Study B is offered to finalists, suggesting that students should have a fairly comprehensive understanding of IR theory. The aims of both modules are to examine the effectiveness of the UN's institutional responses to conflict and crises, taking into account exogenous and endogenous factors that determine the international security institution's schizophrenic behavior. The curriculum design of both, therefore, requires that teachers adopt a pluralist and critical pedagogy so that students can evaluate competing theoretical accounts of the UN's role in maintaining peace and security.

The structures of each module are also remarkably similar to one another and align well with Carlson's objectives. The modules begin with a historical metanarrative of the origin and evolution of the UN and reform of institutional bodies, notably the Security Council and the General Assembly, in relation to decolonization, the rising influence of states from the global south, and regional powers. The second part of the two modules focuses on how the UN's institutional agenda has deepened and broadened in response to the changing security environment and the shift toward conceptualizing security as "human security" (within the third world), and this is the entire focus of semester two in Case Study B. In Case Study A, the curriculum is condensed to just one and a half semesters to free up space for a "mini module" on nongovernmental organizations convened by a different lecturer. This leaves little space to debate and theorize the depth of power relations within the UN system. Due to the larger number of students taking Case Study A (on average 60–70), departmental policy dictates that the three seminar tutors follow the same lesson plans to ensure consistency in learning experience. The structure of each week is predetermined and outlined in the module handbook, thereby restricting opportunities to introduce less mainstream pedagogic approaches. Case Study B is taught in one class, allowing the course convener greater flexibility.

Within the first three weeks, both modules incorporate one session on the theoretical paradigms deemed most relevant for analyzing institutions. These are Realism, Liberalism, New Institutionalism, and Constructivism, and they are expected to be applied throughout the course during lectures, simulations, workshop exercises, and in classroom dialogues. The four dominant theoretical paradigms are incorporated to cover the spectrum of macro- and micro-level analyses of institutions, and organizational and political change (or stasis) within them. The centrality of agency-structure debates in New Institutionalism and Constructivism is particularly valuable when analyzing change brought on by decolonization and global inequalities. Yet, with no engagement with post-colonial IR theories, white privilege is reproduced in the pedagogic encounter.

Since critical pedagogy does not rule out the use of alternative theoretical paradigms, if a student wishes to study the UN using a different paradigm—such as a particular strand of feminism—they may do so. After all, students are taught the "module on gender" prior to taking these two modules, and are therefore arguably equipped, at the very least, with the basic theoretical tools to apply a gendered perspective. In this sense, there is an implicit assumption that a feminist theoretical approach can be used, that students have choice, and that students should feel empowered to adopt whatever theoretical paradigm they wish—both in classroom dialogues and in assignments. That said, in practice, adopting a theoretical paradigm that is not regularly applied in a module can be quite a high risk choice, and one that only the most engaged or politically motivated students in the class are likely to take. The majority of students feel more comfortable using the module's curriculum in assignments.

Gender issues are integrated into the two modules in very controlled ways. Mapping the presence and absence of gendered bodies helps to illustrate this. During the first semester, the only visible person within the UN system itself is the (male) Secretary General, described as a decision-maker, leader, bureaucrat, and norm entrepreneur. All other people that work within and interact with the UN system are invisible, despite emphasis that institutions can be conceptualized as social networks. There is no theorizing about how the institution itself is gendered, nor how inter-sectional forms of discrimination that cut across race, class, age, gender, sexuality, ethnicity, and dis/ability play out in institutional contexts.

In both modules, gendered bodies come into view in the second semester, when the modules focus on the programs of work delivered by the UN's specialized agencies, such as the topics on the UN's protection agenda (for example peacekeeping) and the institution's focus on facilitating human security (through achieving the targets of the Millennium Development Goals, now Sustainable Development Goals). At best, the well-rehearsed (colonialist) liberal feminist narrative about passive and helpless black and brown women in need of being saved from black and brown toxic masculinities is mobilized.

This focus, which incorporates dialogue on the implementation of United Nations Security Council Resolution 1325 (Women, Peace and Security), appears to open up space for students to adopt a feminist standpoint—for instance, by utilizing feminist reconceptualizations of security along a "continuum of violence"—but this paradoxically reinforces the positioning of gender issues as only relevant to the UN's external program of work. Concurrent with the controlled presence of gender issues, there is a silencing of feminist paradigms such as third wave feminisms that set out to disrupt neoliberal governance feminism located in UN policy discourse, or feminist queer theory that disrupts heternormativity in international relations.

These constraints in the curriculum design determine how the international security institution is conceptualized during the pedagogic encounter. We see the UN "doing gender," but the UN is an unproblematically genderless (not even gender neutral) institution. Women of the global south are protected individuals, but are a-political and disempowered—neither engaged as political actors in localized conflicts, as I have discussed elsewhere, nor visible as (educated/elite) women advisors, consultants, and employees working within UN bureaucracy. Patriarchal orderings of gender, taking account of their varied cultures of origin, and the gendered divisions of labor that structure the neoliberal economic system and the UN are shunned, while a whole tranche of institutional power relations are bypassed.

A false reality is sustained in the configuration of the UN as two kinds of institution, to adapt Inis L. Claude's model. The first institution is a depersonalized collectivity formed by its member states and governed by high politics. This is an accepted zone of conflict and a space constructed out of violent and frictional encounters—as noted in the teaching sessions on intersectional class/race power struggles brought about by decolonization and internal pressures to reform the Security Council. The second institution, driven by the will of the secretariat, is expected to uphold the foundational (liberal) ideals on which the institution was built—notably social justice. It is imaged as a "zone of peace," a virtuous institution working to mitigate gendered zones of conflict "elsewhere" in the world. Despite the application of critical pedagogy, the curriculum design of both modules sustains white privilege and reproduces a repressive internal logic that reinforces the UN's neoliberal gender order.

The institutional neoliberal gender order can be observed in the decision to create a separate specialized agency—UN Women—to support delivery of the UN's external program of work, while giving the agency limited authority to facilitate systemwide gender-sensitive reform within the UN. It came into public view in October 2016 when the UN selected Wonder Woman as the much-needed role model to promote the UN's women's empowerment campaign. The UN's decision to select a white, American woman wearing an overly sexualized super-heroine costume generated widespread criticism for sending out all the wrong messages about what kinds of female bodies can be empowered—and what empowerment looked like once embodied. Some 40,000 people signed a petition, allegedly drawn up by women on the UN's payroll, and the campaign was dropped two months later.

This leads to the essay's final question. How do undergraduate modules on the UN socialize male and female students as future employees of institutions? Deconstructing the gendered logics of undergraduate modules enables us to examine what kind of consciousness students are expected to develop through the pedagogic encounter. The repressive logics of the two modules, which promote and legitimize the UN's neoliberal gender order, socialize male and female students to accept the current state of patriarchy of neoliberal institutions and existing gendered divisions of labor within them. They function as a disciplining tool. Those students who choose to adopt a feminist perspective are encouraged to develop a conservative, neoliberal consciousness and the skills to "do gender work," rather than a more radical consciousness required to transform social reality. This belies Carlson's hope for a creative, resourceful future generation to solve existing global issues. For those male and female students who choose not to adopt a feminist perspective, the modules teach students, in the words of Sara Ahmed, "to learn not to notice" the normalization of violence in institutions. As future employees, students develop the ability to screen out bodies and performances that threaten institutions. They learn to perform as required of institutions—asking critically engaged questions but not asking awkward questions that might undermine the authority of the institution and jeopardize their positions as employees.

F eminist scholars of critical pedagogy who draw on Gur-Ze'ev and Friere, such as Kathleen Weiler, contend that intersectional feminist teaching "contains the possibility of transformative work" in its ability to raise the consciousness of students; disrupt the reproduction of sexual divisions of labor within the classroom and in curriculums, and promote democratic relationships and alternative value systems. Pedagogic encounters that address intersectional forms of discrimination do not simply bring identity politics into the study of international institutions. Refusing to privilege any social category, they disrupt the repressive knowledge claims that conceal the UN's internal violent practices of normalization, perpetrated through the informal and formal rules of the institution, and through the behaviors and performances of UN staff. As Sara Ahmed observes, "the personal is structural." To study how international power relations are reproduced through the UN's bureaucracy and through the experiences of individual staff, make the frictional, sometimes violent encounters on which the UN is built and survives palpable. It shatters the ideational image of the institution's bureaucracy as a zone of peace, pushes for systemwide transformation, and compels a rethink about how the UN system should function. Such pedagogic encounters contradict the intentions of Carlson, who believed educational courses provide public relations opportunities to secure the UN's legitimacy.

I now reflect on the feminist pedagogic practices I have used when teaching Case Study B. In my experience of working in Politics and IR departments that are resistant to feminism, there is often an unspoken expectation that feminist scholars should embrace patriarchal pedagogy in their teaching of mainstream IR modules, and reserve feminist praxis for specialized gender modules or their own research. There is a fine balance between ensuring that I, a white British feminist teacher, am not repressed and silenced, nor unwittingly reproduce white privilege during the pedagogic encounter, and preventing the disengagement of students who do not choose to adopt a feminist standpoint. Yet, I have found that by bringing students on board as partners in creating the pedagogic encounter, intersectional feminist interventions into the existing curricula can help to disrupt older patterns of teaching and empower students from diverse backgrounds.

I use Carlson's article as a teaching aid to demonstrate how B.A. curricula have an internal logic capable of reproducing repressive hierarchies of power. I engage students by encouraging them to critically evaluate how knowledge about the UN is (re)produced in the classroom environment. I explain that unless students themselves, and I the teacher, bring our political and theoretical perspectives drawn from personal experiences and histories into our discussions of the UN, we will be at risk of reproducing the neoliberal logic the UN seeks to promote. I remind students that a plethora of theoretical paradigms, including feminism, postcolonialism, and Marxism provide important insights into how institutions function. As an exercise to support this, each week two students must source a relevant news/current affairs article that incites a reaction in them—either positively or negatively—in order that they may share their political and theoretical opinions with the group.

I introduce Feminist Institutionalism, which accounts for multilevel power relations within institutions, as a fifth theoretical paradigm early on in the module. This intervention provides students interested in feminist perspectives with the opportunity to further build on the foundational "week on gender" and specialist gender courses. Yet, since Feminist Institutionalism both counters and responds to New Institutionalism, as Fiona Mackay et al. suggest, the paradigm generates dialogue across the different theoretical approaches and enriches the student's understanding of new institutionalism—the only theory of which students do not have prior knowledge. I also draw on the wealth of academic literature produced by feminist scholars that broach structure-agency debates, formal and informal institutions, and continuity and change through a gendered lens. This includes research on transnational networks; Martha Finnemore, Kathryn Sikkink, Jackie True, and Mona Krook's theorizing of norm dynamics; Hillary Charlesworth's analysis of gender mainstreaming across the UN's specialized bodies and Soumita Basu's compelling study of the appropriation of the Women, Peace, and Security agenda in the foreign policy of member states. This intervention has made the module reading list more gender and race equitable.

Contemporary case studies help students observe how violence and coercion operate through the UN's bureaucracy. The appointment of the Secretary General in 2016, and the #SheMatters campaign led by the campaign group Equality Now, which raised the profile of women candidates, is one such example. Exploring how the campaign evolved via transnational networks and the international media, how female and male candidates performed during live debates, and examining the final voting outcome in relation to geopolitics and decision making within the Security Council succeeds in deconstructing the artificial divide between the two UNs. A second case study on Secretary-General Antonio Guterres's support for the #HeforShe campaign explores political implications of silencing and excluding individuals, and students observe how the lesbian, gay, bisexual, and transgender (LGBT) community has criticized the UN's failure to recognize gender fluidity within the institution, as does a third case study on the refusal of the majority of Human Rights Council members to accept LGBT rights. In the second semester, students draw causal links between institutional violence and the implementation of the UN's external program of work. For example, peacekeeper sexual exploitation and abuse is an institutional failing at all levels of the UN, not simply a failing of militaries from predominantly the global south.

The intention of these feminist pedagogic interventions is not to "engender" teaching about the UN per se, but to offer up alternative possibilities that enrich the study of international security institutions and teach students how as prospective employers and employees they can facilitate social justice.

ACKNOWLEDGMENT

This essay was first presented as a paper at the "Gender and the Political Academy" conference, University of Cambridge, May 2, 2017.

RECOMMENDED READINGS

Ahmed, Sara. 2017. *Living and Feminist Life*. Durham/London: Duke University Press.

Carson, Anne-Marie. 2013. "Is It Still Necessary to Teach About the United Nations?" UN Chronical. Accessed August 15, 2017. https://unchronicle.un.org/article/it-still-necessary-teach-about-united-nations.

Claude, Inis. 1996. "Peace and Security: Prospective Roles for the Two United Nations." *Global Governance*. 2, 289–98.

Craig, John. 2012. "What (if Anything) is Different about Teaching and Learning in Politics?" In *Teaching Politics and International Relations*, edited by Cathy Gormley-Heenan and Simon Lightfoot. Basingstoke, UK: Palgrave Macmillan.

Gur-Ze'ev, Ilan. 1998. "Toward a Nonrepressive Critical Pedagogy." *Education Theory, Fall* 48 (4):463–86.

Holmes, Georgina. 2013. *Women and War in Rwanda: Gender, Media and the Representation of Genocide*. London/New York: I. B. Tauris.

Mackay, Fiona, Meryl Kenny, and Louise Chappell. 2010. "New Institutionalism through a Gender Lens: Towards a Feminist Institutionalism?" *International Political Science Review* 31 (5):573–88.

Rowley, Christina, and Shepherd Laura. 2012. "Contemporary Politics: Using the 'F' Word and Teaching Gender in International Relations." In *Teaching Politics and International Relations*, edited by Cathy Gormley-Heenan and Simon Lightfoot. Basingstoke, UK: Palgrave Macmillan.

Weiler, Kathleen. 2002. *The Critical Pedagogy Reader*, edited by Antonia Darder, Rodolf D. Torres and Marta P. Baltodano. New York/London: Routledge.

Taking a Stand (or a Seat) in the Peace Studies Classroom

KYLE B. T. LAMBELET

Teaching peace and war is an inherently normative exercise. By normative I merely mean that by using words like peace, human rights, justice, and violence, words that are the bread and butter of peace studies, we are always already using a moral vocabulary. And the normative nature of our discipline is not limited to our language. Many of us teach because we want to make the world more peaceful and less violent, and many of our students take our classes with similar motivations. We bring our norms with us to the classroom, as do our students.

These normative commitments, however, are not uniform. Even those of us who are committed to making the world more peaceful and less violent often disagree about how to get there. Should external actors intervene in internal armed conflicts in order to stop open violence? And if yes, how should they intervene? What is the role of international institutions in ensuring justpeace? Can military means be used to create the conditions for justice? Or should we use nonviolent mechanisms of civil resistance if we seek a democratic outcome? These are all questions of means. We can respond to some of these questions empirically with an understanding of what has worked historically, but the fitting together of means and ends is an act of prudence that is irreducibly normative.

Beyond questions of means, some of our students will rightly question whether making the world more peaceful and less violent is a good end at all or, more modestly, whether it is possible for us to achieve it. This is a more radical questioning of the basis of our craft and compels us to consider what the goal of teaching peace and war ought to be. Regardless of how we resolve these questions, the fact that our field is morally committed inevitably impacts our pedagogy. But how?

In my course "Ethics of War, Peace and Revolution," my primary goal is that students take responsibility for their own moral and political commitments regarding violence. Students come to my class with a wide spectrum of already formed (in some cases informed, half-formed, or deformed) normative commitments regarding both the means and ends of peace and war. My principle purpose is not to change their minds, although this sometimes happens. My pedagogical end, rather, is that they take responsibility for their commitments, whatever they may be.

Peace educator Betty A. Reardon argues that taking responsibility is the essential active peacemaking capacity in her classic *Comprehensive Peace Education*. She identifies two aspects of responsibility: responsibility for our complicity in systems of violence and responsibility to the other. In my classroom, taking responsibility means that students are held accountable for the implications of their moral and political commitments, especially how those commitments impact the neighbor, the enemy, and the marginalized. I provide a number of opportunities for taking responsibility, in Reardon's language both responsibility for and to. Most basically, I encourage students to consider the practical implications of their views of peace and war in the concrete production of violence through our in-class discussions and case studies.

I also require students to present an "In the News" assignment in which they apply the concepts of the course to a particular case of their own choosing. This exercise achieves a number of pedagogical goods—allowing students to pursue their own interests, to test the concepts of the course in real time, and to come to specific judgments that they must justify to their peers. But in each case, whether discussions, case studies, "In the News" presentations, or other assignments, my ultimate purpose is to create the conditions for students to take responsibility for their commitments regarding violence and to articulate their responsibility to others.

The taking of responsibility presents a pedagogical challenge: do I demonstrate for my students how to take responsibility by articulating my own commitments in the classroom, in other words by taking a stand, or do I encourage them to take responsibility by creating the deliberative space for them to come to their own conclusions and thus taking a seat? This question presumes two models of teaching, each of which, I will argue, has an important role in peace pedagogy. Each model proposes a different way of using the power and position of the instructor and, as such, each will be appropriate in different institutional and learning contexts.

Before elaborating the two models, let me be clear on what these pedagogical modes share. As models of peace pedagogy, both share an assumption that the instructor does not have a monopoly on knowledge, experience, or truth, but that, as Paolo Friere famously argued, students enter with something to teach as well as something to learn. Thus, both reject the "banking model" that presumes that students are in our classrooms to receive a transmission of knowledge from us, the instructors.

Moreover, as models of peace pedagogy, both share a common goal that students, paraphrasing Ian M. Harris, not only learn about peace but learn for peace. The goal of teaching is that students are transformed: whether by deepening their understanding of commitments already held or revising their commitments in light of new information. Peace education is in this way akin to critical theory. As Karl Marx argued in his eleventh thesis on Feuerbach, the goal of such theorizing is not merely to interpret the world but to change it.

Finally, as should be clear from what I have already written, both models are inescapably normative. They are freighted with moral assumptions about the good and the right, about what a human is and should be, and about how we should organize our common life. Again, this normative orientation is basic to the task of peace education and will play a role in our pedagogy regardless of our instructional disposition.

I t is important to note these commonalities because it is, at times, too easy to label one model or the other as undermining the foundational purposes of peace education. Both taking a stand and taking a seat can emerge from these common commitments of peace pedagogy. These pedagogical first principles, however, do not give concrete guidance on our own position and power as instructors, and this is the problem I wish to consider in the remainder of this essay. If we want students to take responsibility for their commitments and to the other, how should we posture ourselves as teachers?

One way that peace educators invite students to take responsibility is by taking a stand on particular issues of concern. This first model will come naturally to those who started out engaging the task of teaching as peace actors. While still in line with Freire's liberatory, dialogical education, this model pursues education as formation. The instructor demonstrates to students how to take responsibility by taking responsibility herself. In doing so, she holds herself up as an exemplar, or a paradigm, for students to follow. Alternatively, the instructor might include exemplars on the syllabus, people who have been effective peace-builders, nonviolent actors, or just warriors. When taking a stand for more peace and less violence the assumption of this model is that students will have been already exposed to numerous exemplars that justify violence, the instructor is thereby offering a dialogic counterpoint to the dominant culture.

To say this model pursues education as formation is merely to indicate what the ancient Greek philosopher Aristotle taught, that in order to know how to live an excellent life, we need people of excellence that we can follow. Exemplars are an indispensable means of accessing moral excellence, and in the case of peace studies, they help us see that more peaceful and less violent lives and societies are possible. In our understanding of peace and war exemplars play an epistemic role, meaning they help us to know something we did not know before. If you are like me you can probably remember teachers who took a stand on controversial political and social issues and thereby changed the way you thought and acted. For me, these teachers modeled courage to think freely and critically and to take a path of greater resistance. These teachers who have taken a stand have been critical to my own formation.

The danger of such a pedagogical model is that students will not take responsibility for their own commitments but will attempt to discover the instructor's commitments and tailor their class performance to earn a better grade. Rather than taking responsibility, they might merely mimic the instructor (in homage or parody). Inevitably, students will want to know, what do you really think? And in asking, they hope to discover the correct stand to take and thereby how to ace the final. This may serve learning as students outside the power structure of the classroom might find they take up the arguments, ideas, and practices they mimicked inside the classroom. But, it also relies heavily on the power differential between teacher and student, exemplar and follower. At its most extreme, such a model can devolve into an authoritarian pedagogy in which students merely conform themselves to the instructor and will be at a loss when they encounter complex problems of peace and war beyond the classroom.

Against the excesses of this model, some peace educators choose to take a seat. This alternative is an "objective" teaching model in which multiple views are presented and the instructor remains aloof from claiming any particular position. Formation in this model here is secondary to a commitment to the freedom of the student for curiosity and intellectual inquiry. The goal of the instructor here is not to model taking responsibility but to cultivate a deliberative space in which students are encouraged to take responsibility themselves for their moral and political commitments toward violence.

If taking a stand can be linked, at least in part, to Aristotle's ethics of exemplarity, taking a seat draws inspiration from the teacher of Aristotle's teacher Socrates. Socrates, of course, led with questions, a process that philosophers call *elenchus* (a Greek term meaning refutation). The disposition of the instructor here is not to take one side or the other, but to pursue truth through the elenctic process of questions and critique. Again, we can all likely recall teachers who were intentionally coy about their own commitments in class but who always seemed to come to the defense of the side of the dialogue (or argument) that was weakest. For me, these teachers patiently encouraged me to develop my own voice and come to my own judgments. Teachers who have taken a seat have modeled a respect for critical inquiry that I have integrated into my own teaching vocation.

Yet this model too has its dangers. One is that the instructor's commitments still set the terms of dialogue but do so covertly without explicit naming. It pretends a naiveté about the dynamics of power that are part of any formal educational setting. At the end of the day, the instructor sets the syllabus (even one that is flexible), regulates classroom speech and behavior, and gives marks. Some of these dynamics might be mitigated somewhat in movement or nonprofit educational settings, but they never disappear. And, even if we can disable some of the power imbalances that characterize the teaching venture, a second danger is that students may merely leave with a sense that there are many options, but fail to take responsibility for how they might decide among those options. Rather than taking responsibility within an ethos of respectful pluralism, students may leave such a class with a blithe relativism that fails to honor the normative urgency of our subject matter.

So, how should we invite students to take responsibility for the life and death decisions that are the subject of our classes on peace and war? Should we take a stand and thereby model for students how to take responsibility? Or should we take a seat and cultivate the space for deliberative inquiry in which students can take responsibility themselves? In this short essay I will not venture to give a definitive one-size-fits-all answer to these very important questions. In fact, to offer a definitive answer would itself be part of the problem. My proposal is rather that taking a stand and taking a seat are two pedagogical strategies that should be prudentially deployed in our classrooms.

Rather than promoting one or the other pedagogical model I think both require a constant attention to the relationship between responsibility, power, and position. Responsibility for the impact of our moral and political commitments and responsibility to the neighbor, enemy, and marginalized require attention to power and position both in the classroom and beyond. Ultimately the positions we take in the classroom should be informed by a sober analysis of our personal and institutional power in relation to the students.

All teachers regardless of institutional context or subject location set the terms of the teaching environment. This is an act of power that we should own self-critically. While there can be a high degree of mutuality across formal and informal educational venues, formal education requires heightened attention to institutional power. When we teachers are developing syllabi, crafting lesson plans, and grading assignments we are exercising the power of our office and using a mix of disciplinary and incentive structures to cultivate student learning. I am not arguing that this is a bad thing. Rather, these are formative structures that can be used and abused and we need to pay attention to the way in which those powers are working.

We need to pay attention not only to our institutional power, but also the power that comes from our various subject positions. As a white, cis-gendered, heterosexual, male, U.S. citizen, I have significant privileges afforded to me simply on the basis of those markers. I have a responsibility to my students to pay close attention to how my subject position influences the construction of our classroom ethos. That responsibility will look different for differently located persons, but the responsibility to attend to the power of subject position will remain.

Attending to institutional and personal power is important not only for instructors, but also in relation to students. The decision of whether to take a stand or take a seat will change based on the program of students, whether the course is a general education requirement or an upper-level elective, whether students are typically first-generation college students, majority male or female, or any other number of considerations.

I raise all of these to say that whether to take a stand or take a seat is a prudential decision that must take into account our institutional and personal power in relation to our students. I have made different decisions in different institutional contexts. For example, when teaching a general studies requirement to non-major undergraduates, I have tended to take a seat. In doing so, I seek to allow students with whom I have a high power differential the space to develop their own views and positions. Alternatively, when teaching masters-level professional students in upper-level electives, I am more apt to take a stand. For these students I acknowledge that they are more ready to critique my stand and offer alternatives. Which pedagogical strategy I use changes based on institutional context and the quality of my relationship with my students. It also changes with shifts in the wider political discourse. When other contrasting voices are readily available to students, such as during a hotly contested election, I have felt freer to add my voice to the mix, regardless of institutional location, knowing that students will have many arguments ready at hand to resist with, should they choose to do so.

When considering which pedagogical strategy to employ we might ask ourselves a series of evaluative questions. When taking a stand, we might ask: Have I given students the resources and the permission to disagree with me? What other exemplars have I offered to students beyond myself? In what ways will my institutional role as instructor distort students' capacities to think critically about my stand? When taking a seat, we might ask: Have students been confronted with the urgency of decision? Have I analyzed reflexively the covert arguments in the syllabus? And have I made those arguments clear to students? Have I taken the risks that I am asking my students to take?

The paradox of peace education is that we need both pedagogical strategies. The world that we want is one in which we take a seat and listen deeply to one another, exchange ideas, and acknowledge difference with mutual respect, and do so in a way that is not controlled coercively by any one person. To get to that world, however, we have to take a stand against bigotry and for social justice, pointing out coercion and violence, and modeling conflict transformation. We will need both strategies if we are to create a context in which our students take responsibility for their own commitments and join us in the creation of a world characterized by more peace and less violence.

RECOMMENDED READINGS

Aristotle. 2009. *The Nicomachean Ethics*, edited by Leslie Brown. Translated by David Ross. Oxford, UK: Oxford University Press.

Freire, Paulo. 2000. *Pedagogy of the Oppressed*. (30th anniversary ed.) New York, NY: Continuum.

Harris, Ian M. 1988. *Peace Education*. Jefferson, NC: McFarland.

hooks, bell. 1994. *Teaching to Transgress: Education as the Practice of Freedom*. New York, NY: Routledge.

Marx, Karl, and Friedrich Engels. 1978. "Theses on Feuerbach" in *The Marx-Engels Reader.*, edited by Robert C. Tucker. New York, NY: Norton.

Plato. 1977. *Euthyphro, Apology of Socrates, and Crito*, edited by John Burnet. Oxford, UK: Clarendon Press.

Reardon, Betty. 1988. *Comprehensive Peace Education: Educating for Global Responsibility*. New York, NY: Teachers College Press.

Circle of Praxis Pedagogy for Peace Studies

MIKE KLEIN, AMY FINNEGAN AND JACK NELSON-PALLMEYER

Peace Studies is a burgeoning academic discipline with hundreds of uniquely crafted programs at institutions of higher education around the world. The University of St. Thomas (St. Paul, Minnesota, USA) established a Justice and Peace Studies academic program in the late 1980s. Today, the Department of Justice and Peace Studies offers four concentrations in Conflict Transformation, Leadership for Social Justice, Public Policy and Analysis, and Generalist, as well as a minor in Justice and Peace Studies and a new minor in Peace Engineering, designed to complement a B.S. in Engineering. In our experience, the cornerstone of Peace Studies is pedagogy: the theory and practice of how we learn and how we teach.

The Circle of Praxis pedagogy is the foundation for our program and it continues to inform how, what, and why we teach and learn. The Circle of Praxis encompasses four interactive and complementary dimensions to compel learners to embrace a method of examination and engagement: Insertion, Descriptive Analysis, Normative Analysis, and Action Planning. Woven together in an iterative process of action and reflection, the Circle of Praxis guides transformative education toward both personal agency and structural change to promote justice and peace.

The Circle of Praxis is rooted in twentieth-century Latin American liberation movements and continues to be adopted—and adapted—in diverse settings around the world. Although it reflects other change processes with long histories (that is, "observe, judge, act"), we trace our roots through Latin American liberation theology of Guttierez, Ellacuria, and Sobrino, back to the groundbreaking pedagogical work of Paulo Freire in *Pedagogy of the Oppressed, Education for Critical Consciousness*, and other works. Freire's pedagogical work has been carried forward by critical pedagogues and social movement educators in formal, nonformal, and informal educational settings. We draw on Freire's invitation to collectively examine what is given and what is constructed, to identify contradictions and develop critical consciousness about inequities and injustices that are assumed to be normal. We utilize the transformative educational framework of the Circle of Praxis that moves from experiential engagement with the social world to social analysis in the classroom as a community of teachers and learners. The aim of Freirean-inspired education—and our program in Justice and Peace Studies—is critical consciousness in the service of collective action to challenge, resist, and construct a more just and peaceful society.

Jack was introduced to the Circle of Praxis in the mid-1970s by Gustavo Gutierrez, a liberation theologian from Peru who was a teacher, friend, and mentor. Gutierrez and others adapted the liberating methodology pioneered by Paulo Freire to their efforts to transform the Church and unjust social systems and structures in Latin America. Historically, the Church arrived through colonialism and alongside the conquest, armed with guns and a theology of obedience to authority, personal salvation, and heavenly reward. For generations, the Church functioned as a willing instrument of the powerful and a complicit partner in the systematic oppression of the poor.

Throughout the 1980s, Jack witnessed how impoverished but well-organized peasant and urban communities in Nicaragua and El Salvador employed the Circle of Praxis in a liberating process of educational and societal transformation. Jack was also impacted profoundly by the example of the Jesuit-run University of Central America (UCA) in San Salvador where the Circle of Praxis was at the heart of the university's mission and curriculum. Not surprisingly, most universities worldwide tell prospective students that attending their university is the key to personal success. Given that universities exist in a society rife with structural injustices and unequal opportunities, the idea that a university will help a student succeed even in a very unjust world is implicit to the promise. The UCA's explicit goal was education for transformation in the context of profound injustices in Salvadoran society and a U.S.-sponsored dirty war. Six Jesuit priests who led and inspired the UCA, some of whom Jack knew, were killed by U.S.-trained soldiers in November 1989 because they persistently used their voices to promote greater peace and justice, and sought to equip students with the necessary knowledge and skills to address and transform societal injustices.

The liberation thrust of the Circle of Praxis pedagogy has transformative possibilities that include, but extend well beyond, theological, church, or social justice struggles in Latin America. Our program's founder, Rev. David W. Smith, placed the Circle of Praxis at the heart of Justice and Peace Studies where we believe it belongs. He practiced this transformative pedagogy as he built the program in the 1990s. We continue to articulate the application of this pedagogy in our curriculum and classroom, and now offer this essay as a concise introduction and overview of our approach to teaching justice and peace.

Step one in the Circle of Praxis Pedagogy is Insertion/Immersion. In this pedagogy, the starting point for the pursuit of knowledge generally is not an academic probe of ideas and theories (or for theology, specifically, a targeted study of God) but rather, it begins in direct or indirect encounters with people who are oppressed or marginalized from the dominant power structures, struggling to survive, and overcoming the brutalities of unjust social systems. Insertion or immersion—the first spoke in the Circle of Praxis—is essential for teachers and students alike, because we can be captive to our limited experiences and the inadequacies of our inherited worldviews. Our social location, including but not limited to national identity, gender, social class, and race largely determines what we see and do not see, what we think about and do not think about, what we question and do not question, and what we know and do not know. Indeed, what we see, think, question, and know is profoundly influenced or determined by whether we are beneficiaries or victims of unjust systems.

Insertion/immersion is fraught with ethical and moral dilemmas for peace studies as we try to engage with people in vulnerable situations who may have faced recent or generational exploitation, and people whose stories may have been previously absent and now risk being appropriated. Direct insertion/immersion in peace studies (through service-learning, community engagement, or immersion trips) and indirect insertion/immersion (through written accounts, documentary films, or guest speakers) must, at least, do no harm. Such experiential engagement can be a dynamic component in transformational learning, but we have learned to also consider the expressed interests of people facing oppression, marginalization, or violence before the needs of educators or students. We have also learned that insertion/immersion into oppression should not be constructed as experiences with "vulnerable people" that our learners must go off campus to encounter; indeed, many in our own community of learners know too well the intimate realities of violence, marginalization, and injustice. Ideally, we seek to create spaces for all to reflect on these lived experiences and build relationships of mutuality in ongoing and sustainable partnerships.

Insertion/immersion is exemplified in Amy's Conflict Analysis and Transformation course through student participation in Soliya's Connect Program. This eight-week online dialogue allows students to engage in small group facilitated conversations through video conferencing with other university students from North America, Europe, the Middle East, northern Africa, and Asia. The focus of this track III diplomatic dialogue is exploring the relationship between "the West" and "the Muslim World." In Amy's estimation, students learn not just about conflict occurring "out there" in the world, but they actively participate in a dynamic conflict transformation effort in which they are a central party. In a contemporary American context, rampant with acute Islamophobia and where communities are socialized to dehumanize "the other," the Soliya insertion/immersion effort provides opportunities for students to build peer relationships across the Muslim majority world and beyond.

Insertion/immersion into the experience and stories of people facing marginalization, oppression, or violence decenters our worldview to help us see from the perspective of those most in need of justice and peace. This conscious choice at the beginning of our pedagogy is intended to cultivate empathy, to challenge our vision of "common sense" assumptions rooted in bias or privilege, and to problematize contradictions between our beliefs and experience. Insertion/immersion grounds our analysis but does not consider experience authoritative in and of itself. By necessity, it leads to the second spoke in the Circle of Praxis.

Step two in the Circle of Praxis Pedagogy is Descriptive Analysis. Descriptive analysis refers to rigorous academic efforts that seek to expose and understand causal factors and unjust systems responsible for hunger, poverty, violence, war, and social injustice. This second spoke in the Circle of Praxis posed serious challenges to theologians who approached the study of God divorced from the actual experience and rigorous study of poverty. Its causal factors, including unjust political, economic, and social systems and structures are frequently downplayed or ignored. So, too, must Peace Studies transcend the objectivity advocated in many academic circles to engage what Johann Galtung called "the diagnosis-prognosis-therapy triangle."

Descriptive analysis provides important opportunities for students and educators to move from the grounded experience of insertion/immersion to interdisciplinary analysis through the social sciences. This second spoke in the Circle of Praxis commits us to rigorous academic study of root causes, unjust structures, and unequal power relationships. It begs learners to inquire, who is making effective decisions in a social context? Who is benefitting from the decisions made? And who is paying the costs of these decisions? In many cases, descriptive analysis illuminates how structural violence is operating in context.

As a discipline, Justice and Peace Studies and similar programs are nonpartisan but unapologetically political, inquiring about how power operates in systems, institutions, and among populaces. Commonly articulated goals of Peace Studies include ending or preventing wars; resolving entrenched conflicts without violence; building peaceable societies that are just, sustainable, and equitable; and addressing the root causes of many social, political, and economic problems. In order to pursue these goals and undertake descriptive analysis with integrity, Justice and Peace Studies requires an interdisciplinary approach that helps break down academic silos common within many university systems. At St. Thomas, Justice and Peace Studies requires a strong academic core of foundational courses in the field, but it also draws on insights, knowledge, and inspiration from diverse disciplines within the social sciences: psychology, sociology, political science, international studies, economics, social work, gender studies, cultural studies, and more.

One concrete example of how Justice and Peace Studies realizes descriptive analysis is in our annual World Café event that brings together multiple undergraduate disciplines to address a contemporary social issue (for example apparel supply chains, the HIV/AIDS pandemic, fossil fuels, and climate change). Faculty exchanges help students analyze the issue from different disciplinary lenses in the classroom. Then 300+ students gather in a single evening to engage in focused, mixed-discipline, small group conversations to compare and contrast understandings and wrestle with different analyses of causes and solutions. This cross-disciplinary educational analysis previews the cross-sector professional work they will need to undertake for sustainable peacemaking, peacekeeping, and peacebuilding.

Step three in the Circle of Praxis Pedagogy is Normative Analysis. After we take intentional steps to experience and see the world in new ways (insertion/immersion), and after we demonstrate an unflinching determination to understand causal factors drawing on the best of the various social sciences (descriptive analysis), we are ready for serious reflection about values and vision. The Circle of Praxis pedagogy would be incomplete with questioning our assumptions and judgments in the learning process.

The starting point for normative analysis is recognition that the reality of human suffering, massive poverty, inequality, environmental degradation, oppression, hunger, war, and violence scream out for an honest assessment and radical reassessment of the value and faith systems that allow, support, or nurture unjust systems. Normative analysis fits particularly well in the Peace Studies Programs of religiously identified colleges or universities with a mission that speaks of compassion, the common good, or altruistic aims. We contend that normative analysis should be a vital component of all Peace Studies programs, including those situated within secular institutions. Our reasoning is simple: Unjust political, economic, and societal systems and structures are consequences of deeply

TEACHING PEACE AND WAR 155

flawed value systems that must be challenged and changed. Personal and societal values rooted in religious teachings, cultural narratives, national mythologies, social systems, and/or dominant secular values and norms lead to and reinforce unjust policies, practices, and systems. Normative analysis promotes recognition that better policies leading to greater peace and justice often depend on a profound shift in values.

In Mike's Leadership for Social Justice class, students engage the Normative Analysis step by exploring the implications of problem-based and asset-based work for social justice. They examine stories that frame poor communities as problems and poor people as victims to be helped or fixed by outside intervention. Students compare these stories with examples of capacity-building work that promotes voice, decision making, and collective action for personal and social agency. By articulating the values, responsibilities, rights, and outcomes of different approaches to social justice, students learn to identify conflicting worldviews that frustrate collaboration or prevent reconciliation. As they develop their own profiles of leadership for social justice for the course, they employ critical theory to illuminate intersectional identities and the complex power dynamics of interlocking privileges and oppressions.

Normative analysis builds on the critical, interdisciplinary descriptive analysis of our initial insertion/immersion experience. We analyze values that often remain unexamined, and problematize underlying biases and assumptions that color or distort our descriptive analysis. Our understanding through the social sciences may be rooted in—and may in turn reproduce— misogyny, colonialism, patriarchy, heteronormativity, and so on. Using tools from theology, philosophy, gender or cultural studies, human rights, and critical theory, the Circle of Praxis calls us to examine our own normative commitments and the normative worldview of others to uncover implicit bias, acknowledge differential values, and evaluate how to best work across our differences to promote justice and peace, to build diverse coalitions around common goals. This stage in the Circle of Praxis also invites us to unleash our imaginations to envision alternative futures and to see ourselves as participants in a vital process of reshaping our world.

Step four in the Circle of Praxis Pedagogy is Action Planning. While critical consciousness is the explicit educational goal, a more just and peaceful world is the practical goal of Justice and Peace Studies. The Circle of Praxis pedagogy helps us achieve both goals. Insertion/immersion helps us see the world in a new way. Descriptive analysis requires vigorous and disciplined academic inquiry of causal factors, including the systemic and structural roots of many social, economic, and political problems. Normative analysis encourages us to reflect deeply on the personal and societal values and visions (and faith in religious settings) that reinforce unjust policies, structures, and systems and on alternative values and visions of society that are needed if we are to build more just and peaceable societies.

This fourth spoke in the Circle of Praxis helps us to embrace our role as responsible change makers. Action planning requires both teacher and student to be accountable for what we learn and know. We are not voyeurs looking in on a world of injustice from afar but protagonists and community members in an ongoing enterprise to work on behalf of greater peace and justice. Accountability through responsible action applies to all areas of our lives including our personal choices, our vocational choices, our social engagements, and our political and public work to build peaceable, just, and sustainable societies, systems, and structures.

The action planning step causes us to pause in our urgent rush to change the world by requiring us to learn and apply effective and ethical strategies and tactics. In Justice and Peace Studies at St. Thomas, we introduce students to the Social Change Wheel to help them conceptualize the range of actions that are part of progressive social change. Through the story of the Montgomery Bus Boycott, we demonstrate how disparate social change strategies can coalesce to advance a more cohesive and robust collective action or social movement. From this historical example, and through this conceptual model, students plan strategic action for social change. For example, when students recognized a contradiction between our university's mission and the conventional coffee it served, and alignment between the principles of fair trade coffee and the principle of Catholic social teaching, they decided to work for institutional change. They used sequential strategies of education and research, community organizing, policy formation through political process, economic analysis, and capacity-building to work with our institution to help align practice to mission and bring fair trade organic coffee sourced by a principled local company—Peace Coffee—to campus.

Past examples helped them imagine new approaches to developing engagements and interventions that attend to the dynamics of power. Thoughtful and reflective action planning starts with a commitment to "do no harm" by anticipating unintended consequences. Then, by accounting for allies and adversaries, one's own social location, resources, and obstacles, action planning focuses on developing individual agency and social capacity, promoting solidarity, building coalitions, imagining alternative solutions, and creating innovative and sustainable structures. Action planning is the component of the Circle of Praxis that extends peace studies into peacebuilding. It also completes the circle, encouraging learners to engage in the next insertion/immersion step. The Circle of Praxis is iterative and continuous, moving us toward ever more effective and ethical learning and action to promote justice and peace.

The Circle of Praxis pedagogy profoundly shapes Justice and Peace Studies at University of St. Thomas. It determines the content of core courses required for a major. It shapes the concentrations we offer within the major. It influences our interdisciplinary partnerships, shapes our internships, frames how we support the development of student leaders, and moved us to develop a carefully crafted vocational discernment seminar for seniors in the major. In our experience, the Circle of Praxis is an essential foundation for Peace Studies because it facilitates transformative education on behalf of tangible work for justice and peace.

Students also appreciate the Circle of Praxis for its concrete and clarifying framework for analysis of contemporary social issues. Our graduating seniors, on their own volition, often draw on the Circle of Praxis in senior capstone and honors projects to make meaning out of complex experiences and to discern their own plan for action. More than a behind-the-scenes pedagogical model, the Circle of Praxis has served our students as a habit of mind and a practical tool for rigorous analysis. As the foundational pedagogical framework that defines our vibrant Justice and Peace Studies program at St. Thomas, we offer it here, knowing it can be meaningful for other programs and institutions as well. We encourage you to adopt the Circle of Praxis as a pedagogical framework, and adapt it to your own particular context. If we can share more of our experiences, or walk with you on that journey, please contact us.

RECOMMENDED READINGS

Ellacuria, Ignacio and Jon Sobrino. 1993. *Mysterium Liberationis: Fundamental Concepts of Liberation Theology*. Maryknoll, NY: Orbis Books.

Finnegan, Amy, Mike Klein, Christopher Michaelson, and Sheneeta White. 2016. "Can Business Help to Cultivate Peace and Wellbeing?" *Business, Peace, and Sustainable Development* 2016 (8):55–69.

Finnegan, Amy, Michelle Morse, Marisa Nadas, and Mike Westerhaus. 2017. "Where We Fall down: Tensions in Teaching Social Medicine and Global Health." *Annals of Global Health* 83 (2):347–55.

Freire, Paulo. 1970. */1990. Pedagogy of the Oppressed*. New York, NY: Continuum.

Freire, Paulo. 1973. *Education for Critical Consciousness*. New York, NY: Continuum.

Galtung, Johann. 1996. *Peace by Peaceful Means: Peace and Conflict, Development and Civilization*. Oslo: International Peace Research Institute.

Gutiérrez, Gustavo. 1973. *A Theology of Liberation: History, Politics, and Salvation*. Translated and Edited by Sister Caridad Inda and John Eagleson. Maryknoll, NY: Orbis Books.

Klein, Mike. 2017. "Institutional Ethnography as Peace Research," in *Ethnographic Peace Research: Approaches and Tensions*, edited by Gearoid Millar. London, UK: Palgrave.

Klein, Mike. 2017. "Social Change Wheel Analysis: Beyond Dichotomies of Charity and Justice," *Civil Rights and Inequalities, Occasional Publication #6*. Boston, MA: CAPA.

Klein, Mike. 2013. "Cell Phones, T-Shirts and Coffee: Codification of Commodities in a Circle of Praxis Pedagogy." *Peace Studies Journal Special Edition: The Business of War and Peace, and the Potential for Education to Play a Transformative Role* 6 (1):31–45.

Klein, Mike. 2007. "Peace Education and Paulo Freire's Method: Towards the Democratization of Teaching and Learning." *Convergence Adult Education Journal* 40 (1-2):187–205.

Smith, David Whitten, and Haasl Mike. 1999. "Justice and Peace Studies at the University of St. Thomas," in *Teaching for Justice: Concepts and Models for Service-Learning in Peace Studies*, edited by Kathleen Maas Weigart and Robin J. Crews. Washington, D.C: American Association for Higher Education.

Soliya. *Connect Program*. Available at <https://www.soliya.net/programs/connect-program>, last accessed: October 1, 2017.

Index

abolition of apartheid 22
abolition of slavery 58
action interventions 28, 31–2, 38, 40
action planning 155–6
Action Research 31
activism 21
Adams, Sam 104
advantages of podcasting 7, 11
aesthetic turn 7–8
affect 98
Africa 82–91
Ahmed, Sara 139
Ahmed, Zahid Shahab 75
Al-Shabaab 88
Alexander, Ronni 1
Alliance for Peacebuilding 130
"alternative facts" 52
Alternative to Violence Project 24–7
ambiguity 45, 92, 99
Ancient Kurdistan 111–12
anti-corruption 32–3
anti-fascism 108
apartheid 22, 25–6
AR *see* Action Research
Arab Spring 87
arch of instability 89
"archaeology of mind" 84
Aristotle 145–6
Armstrong, Karen 75
art-making 14–21
Asad, Talal 69
assessing reliability 50
Attitudes of Teachers in India and Pakistan 75
attunement 92
audio podcasting *see* podcasting pedagogy
Autesserre, Séverine 42
autonomy 11, 110

AVP *see* Alternative to Violence Project
awareness 16–17
Aziz, Khursheed Kamal 75

balanced reporting 6
"banking model" 144–5
baraza 34
Barker, Lt. Col. Frank A., Jr. 49–50
Barnard College 54
Basabose, Jean de Dieu 32–3
Basu, Soumita 140
Baxter, Michelle 75
Bekerman, Zvi 120
belligerence 88
Big Truck that Went By, The 42
Biko, Steve 23, 26
Bjorklund, Stefani 60
Bleiker, Roland 8
Boal, Augusto 17
Boko Haram 88
Bokova, Irina 82
Boston Massacre 103–4
Boulding, Elise 129
Buddhism 69, 71, 92–3
building hopeful pedagogy 24
Butler, Judith 9
bystanderism 42

Cabezudo, Alicia 123
Calley, Lt. William 50
Calvino, Italo 10
Camp David 122
Campbell, Susan 60
capitalism 71
Carlson, Anne-Marie 133, 135–6, 139–40
celebrating war 101
Charlesworth, Hillary 140
Charter for Compassion 75–6
Christianity 69, 71, 116

INDEX

Circle of Praxis 150–58; action planning
    155–6; descriptive analysis 153–4;
    insertion/immersion 152–3; normative
    analysis 154–5
civic responsibility 33
Civil Rights Movement 106, 129
classism 95
Claude, Inis L. 138
climate change 102, 154
Colbeck, Carol 60
Cold War 68, 106
collaboration 31–3, 35, 56–7, 60–67, 88, 93
collectivity 74–5
colonization 20, 96
Combat Action Report 49–50
commercialization 120
common assumptions about religion 71–2
Community World Service 75
compassion 75–6, 154
complicity 144
Comprehensive Peace Education 144
compromise 64
*Conflict and Communication Activity Book,
    The* 63
conflict and engagement 54–9, 68–73; and
    religion 68–73
conflict management pedagogy 60–67
Conflict Map Group Project 60–61
Conflict Mapping 23–4, 27; steps 27–9
Conflict Regulation 60
conflict resolution 17–18, 22–4, 34–6,
    60–67, 77–9
Connect Program 152
Constructivism 136
continuum of violence 137
corruption 32–3
counter-education 134
counterfactuals from hell 38–46
Craig, John 134
creation of agency 24–7
Cremin, Hilary 119
critical concept (de)formation 68, 70–72
critical pedagogy 133–42
critical turn 134
curricula 74–158; Circle of Praxis
    pedagogy 150–58; decolonizing
    practices for Western educators 92–100;
    idealism vs pragmatism 74–81; intrigue
    in Africa 82–91; Iraqi Kurdistan's history
    curricula 110–118; in the peace studies
    classroom 143–9; tangible peace 127–32;
    teaching U.S. history students 101–9;
    transrational peacebuilding education
    119–26; UN, gender, critical pedagogy
    133–42

Daesh *see* Islamic State of Iraq and Syria
de-unification 97
decision making 21, 105
*Declaration of the Rights of Men and
    Citizen* 57–8
decolonizing practices 24, 92–100, 119
deficit model 39
defilement 98
dehumanization 25–6
demoralization 112
descriptive analysis 153–4
diagnosis-prognosis-therapy triangle 153
dialogic learning 28
Dietrich, Wolfgang 124
Different Kind of War Story, A 9
differentiation 84
diligence 62
disconnection 96
*Discourse on the Injustices of the Laws in
    Favour of Men at the Expense of Women*
    57
disempowerment 36, 125
disenfranchisement 94
diversity 61, 84, 122
divide and rule 89, 96
"Do U.N. Interventions Cause Peace?" 43
"doing gender" 137–8
Drezner, Daniel 44

Echavarría, Josefina 119
economic inequality 36
economic stagnation 87
education systems in Pakistan 74–81
El-Malik, Shiera 7, 9
elenchus 146–7
elicitive values 124
Ellacuria, Ignacio 150
emergency law 22
empowerment 36, 125
endemic violence 25–6
ending the Holocaust 108–9
engagement 28, 38, 49, 54–9
English as a second language 112
Enlightenment 57, 68
epistemic violence 119–24
epistemological concerns in intervention
    43–4
epistemological pluralism 125
Equality Now 140–41
essentialism 68–70
ethical concerns in intervention 40–42
ethicist ideology 86
ethics of listening 10, 40
"Ethics of War, Peace and Revolution"
    143–4

INDEX

ethnocentric approaches to peacebuilding 119–20
euphemizing war 101
exoticization 120
experiments in intimacy 7
"expert ignorance" 86
exploitation 23–4, 105, 1441
extremism 76, 82

"fake news" 52
falsification of predictions 43
Fanon, Frantz 23, 96–7
feminism 96, 136
Feminist Institutionalism 140
Fink, L. Dee 61
Finnegan, Amy 152–3
Finnemore, Martha 140
Fog of War 47–53
foundational literature 2
Freire, Paolo 4, 23–4, 28–9, 94, 97–8, 134, 139, 144–5, 150–51
French Revolution 54–9
Frye, Marilyn 95

Galtung, Johan 129, 153
Gbagbo, Laurent 86
GBV *see* gender-based violence
gender 15, 18–19, 133–42
gender equality 18, 117
gender mainstreaming 140
gender-based violence 22, 33
gendered social relations 10, 15
genocide 38–42, 89–90, 108–9
Gestalt psychology 94
"Getting to Know You" survey 61–2
Gilligan, Michael 43
Giroux, Henry 7
Global Campaign for Peace Education 26, 83
Global Peace System 129–32
global politics 71
Global War on Terror *see* War on Terror
glorification of heroes 74
good vs evil 108, 128
grammar of governmentability 86
Great Depression 101
grief 9, 16
group projects for conflict management 60–67
gun violence 84
Gur Ze-Ev, Ilan 120, 134, 139
Gurukahundi massacres 34
Guterres, Antonio 141
Gutiérrez, Gustavo 150–51

Harris, Ian M. 145
#HeForShe 141

Heart of Understanding, The 92–8
hegemonic education 134
Henkeman, Sarah 36
hijacking 22
Hinduism 71
Hirondelle Foundation 6
Hiroshima 20, 105
Hitler, Adolf 108
HIV/AIDS 154
Hollywood 101
Holocaust Museum (U.S.) 41
homophobia 95
hooks, bell 23
hopelessness 24
"hot takes" 44
hubris 45
human costs of war 75
Human Rights Council 141
human rights violations 41–2
human trafficking 18
humanizing the study of peace/war 9, 11
Hurd, Shakman 69

iconoclasm 99
idealism vs pragmatism 74–81
ideas industry 44
Illich, Ivan 120
immaculateness 98
immersion 152–3
immorality 39
impartiality 86–7
imperialism 95, 108
In the Lake of the Woods 48
Inayatullah, Naeem 7
incitement of violence 22
inclusion 15, 19, 66
independence struggle 111
indigenous knowledge 23, 25
individual accountability 61
insertion/immersion 152–3
insiders–outsiders 85–6, 88–9
Institute of Peace (U.S.) 77
inter-being 98
interdependence 67, 89–90
interfaith harmony 77, 90
International Center for Religion and Diplomacy 74
international peace camp 20
International Peace Research Association 26, 129
international security 6
International Youth Day 83
intolerance 75
intrigue of African peace and war curriculum 82–91

intuition 97
Iraq 110–118
Iraqi Kurdistan *see* Kurdistani history curricula
irrationality 56
ISIS *see* Islamic State of Iraq and Syria
Islam 63, 69, 71–2, 74, 77, 89, 110–118
Islamic State of Iraq and Syria 44, 63, 72, 88
Islamification 82–3, 88
Islamophobia 153

Japan 14, 18–20; *see also* Popoki Peace Project
jihad 112, 115
jizya 116
Jobs, Steve 106
Johnson, David 60–61
Johnson, Roger 61
Judaism 71
Juergensmeyer, Mark 69

kamishibai 18–19
Kanwal Sheikh, Mona 69
Katz, Jonathan 42
Kester, Kevin 119, 121–3
Khuankaew, Outporn 94–5, 98
King, Martin Luther 26
King, Martin Luther, Jr. 88, 106, 131
Kiyala, Chrys 34
Klein–Mike 155
Knight, Arletta 61
Kroc Institute for International Peace Studies 131–2
Krook, Mona 140
Kuperman, Alan J. 42
Kurdification 111
Kurdistani history curricula 110–118
KwaZulu-Natal 22

Lawson, James 106
learning about war 19
Lederach, Jean Paul 36, 120, 124–5
lessons of history 2, 38–9
Lewin, Kurt 32
Lewis, John 106
LGBT community 141
liberation psychology 92–5, 98–9
listening skills 6–8, 10–11, 19–20, 63
lived approaches to religion 69–70
Locke, Thomas 56
Lonn, Steven 6
Lopez, George 131
loss 9
Lynch, Cecelia 69

Mabaso, Busi 29
Mackay, Fiona 140
madrassa schooling 76–8, 80
Mahatma Gandhi 26, 131
"Making Education for Peace" 82
Mamdani, Mamood 23
Mandela, Nelson 23, 26, 131
Maphosa, Buhlebenkosi 33–4
March 2011 earthquake 16
marginalization 116
Martín-Baró, Ignacio 93–4
martyrdom 113–15
Marx, Karl 45, 145
Marxism 71, 140
Mbembe, Achille 23
meaningful atrocity prevention 40
mediation 26, 66
Metelits, Claire 89
methodological concerns in intervention 42–3
Mezirow, Jack 23
Michaelsen, Larry 61
militarization 15, 20, 87
Millennium Development Goals 137
mindfulness 94–5
mise-en-scène 6, 8, 11
misogyny 95
mitigation 72
Montgomery Bus Boycott 156
"Moral Hazard of Humanitarian Intervention, The" 42
Morales, Aurora Levins 96
Mount Mary University 54, 57
Muchemwa, Cyprian 34
Muppidi, Himadeep 9
Murder of History 75
Mutambara, Agrippa 87
My Lai massacre 3, 48–52

Naeemia, Jamia 76, 78
Nagasaki 20
Nash, Diane 106
Natal War 22
nationalism 121–4
NATO *see* North Atlantic Treaty Organization
navigating personal conflict 60–61
negative peace 15
Nelson-Pallmeyer, Jack 151
neo-patrimonialism 84
neoliberal gender logic 133
neoliberalism 23–4
neutrality 86–7
New Institutionalism 136
Nhat Hanh, Thich 92–8

INDEX

9/11 68, 104
nonviolence 23, 25, 88, 90, 102, 106–7, 109, 112, 131–2
Nordstrom, Carol 8–9
normalization of violence 139
normative analysis 154–5
Norsworthy, Kathryn L. 94–5, 98
North Atlantic Treaty Organization 39
Nsteane, Gabo 23

Oakley, Barbara 61–2, 64
Obama, Barack 41
objectivity 71, 86–7
O'Brien, Tim 48
open learning 84
oppression 23–4, 28–9, 36, 95, 154
Orsi, Robert 69
ostracization 95
the "other" 34, 97, 153
Ouattara, Alassane 86
outsiders–insiders 85–6, 88–9

Pacifica Graduate Institute 92
Paiman Alumni Trust 79
Pakistan 74–81
Palestine 20–21
Palm, Etta 57
PAR *see* Participatory Action Research
Parks, Rosa 106
Participatory Action Research 31–7
patriarchy 23–4, 28, 94, 117
pax romana 120
peace education 22–30
Peace and Education Development Foundation 77–8
peace and religion 68–73
peace and war in the classroom 1–5
Peace of Westphalia 68
peacebuilding 31–7, 119–24; transrational 119–24
peacemaking 23, 25–6, 34, 43
PEAD Foundation *see* Peace and Education Development Foundation
Pearl Harbor 107–8
pedagogy 6–73; conflict management pedagogy 60–67; PAR for peacebuilding 31–738–46; peace education at a South African university 22–30; podcasting pedagogy 6–13; "Reacting to the Past" pedagogy 54–9; religion, conflict, peace 68–73; teaching with Popoki 14–21; truth, sources, Fog of War 47–53
Pedagogy of the Oppressed 150
peer evaluation 64–5
perpetuation of ethnic superiority 89

personal sense of agency 24–7
peshmergah 113–15
physical violence 22–3
"Pinkville" *see* My Lai massacre
Playback Theatre 17
plural pedagogy 134
podcasting pedagogy 6–13
Poga 16–17
polarization 23
political affiliation 86
political murders 22
political sensibilities 7
Popoki Friendship Story 16
Popoki Peace Project 14–21
Popoki, What Color is Peace? 14
portability 7
posited interventions 39
positive peace 15, 32
post-genocide peace education 89–90
posttraumatic stress disorder 105–6
poverty 23, 84–5, 128, 154
power dynamics 66, 95, 97
Power, Samantha 40, 42
practical peacemaking 25
pragmatism 74–81
privatization 8
privileged language 96–7, 99
Problem from Hell, A 40, 42
problem solving 60–61, 94–5
Prophet Mohammed 112–16
prudence 143
psycho-social approaches to peacebuilding 119–20, 123
PTSD *see* posttraumatic stress disorder

Quran 115

racism 15, 95, 108, 115, 128
radicalism 82, 88–9
Rankin, Janette 105
rape 96
rationalist orthodoxy 133
"Reacting to the Past" 54–9
reactionism 87
Reagan, Ronald 106
realities of war 47, 51–2
Reardon, Betty 123, 144
Rebel in Me, The 97
receptivity 6
reconciliation 114, 117
reducing epistemic violence 119–24
reductionism 98
reflection 31–2, 86–7, 90
reliability 50
religion 68–73

INDEX

religious terrorism 69; *see also* terrorism
rescripting the difficult 10–11
responsibility 147–8
responsible uncertainty 44
restorative justice 34
Revere, Paul 104
Richmond, Oliver 120
Ridenhour, Ronald L. 49–50
right listening 63
right to peace 19, 82
Rösch, Felix 7
Rousseau, Jean-Jacques 56–7
Rowley, Christina 133–4
RTTP *see* "Reacting to the Past"

Saint-Domingue 56, 58
scriptedness 7–8, 11
secularism 71–2
securitization 8–9, 69, 85–6
self-awareness 97
self-criticism 147
self-defense 113
self-determination 111–12
self-reflexivity 96
self-rule 110, 112, 117
Sergenti, Ernesto 43
sex work 18
sexism 95, 108
sexual violence 29, 33
#SheMatters 140–41
Shepherd, Laura 133–4
Shifferd, Kent 129
Sikkink, Kathryn 140
sitting in peace studies classroom 143–9
skepticism 102, 107, 119
slavery 56, 58
Smith, Karl 61
Smith, Rev. David W. 151
Sobrino, Jon 150
Social Change Wheel 156
social contract 57
socialization 23–4, 28
Socrates 146
Soliya 152
Soro, Guillaume 87
source criticism 49
sources 47–53
South Africa 22–30
South–South simulations 121
sovereignty 10
speaking truth to power 95
Spurr, David 96
state hegemony 118
steps of Conflict Mapping 27–9; *see also* Conflict Mapping

stereotyping 10, 75, 116, 122
Stevens, Maurice E. 95
stigmatization 84, 89–90, 95
Stockholm International Peace Research Institute 129
storytelling 18–19
Strausz, Erzsebet 9, 11
"Strengthening Cohesion and Resilience" 78
structural violence 26, 28, 36, 83
studying history in U.S. 101–9
subjectivity 4, 15–16
subjugation 95
suicide bombings 76
Sulh Alhudaibia 114
support scaffolding 64–5
Swat Youth Front (Pakistan) 78–9
Sweden 47–53
Sylvester, Christine 133

Tablet magazine 41
tangible peace 127–32
Tatsine, Yan 89
teaching counterfactuals from hell 38–46
Teaching in Higher Education 122
teaching peace, not war, in U.S. 101–9
teaching peace with Popoki 14–21
teaching religion and peace 68–73
Teasley, Stephanie 6
TED talks 44
Tehrik-i-Taliban 76, 78–9
terrorism 8–9, 18, 69, 76, 85, 101
testimony 8–9
Theatre of the Oppressed 17
theory of securitization 8–9
"toolbox" metaphor in atrocity prevention 40–41
torture 96
trafficking 18
transrational peacebuilding education 119–26
trauma 23–4, 89–90, 95, 105, 121
TRIP survey 44
Trouble with the Congo, The 42
True, Jackie 140
"true" narrative 51
truth 47–53
Tufte, Edward R. 130–31
Tunisian Revolution 87
Tutu, Desmond 23

Ubuntu 86
UCA *see* University of Central America
UN *see* United Nations
UN Chronicle 133, 135
Un roi à l'écoute 10

INDEX

UN Security Resolution 1325 137
UN Security Resolution 2250 82
understanding peace 14–15, 19, 23
unemployment 23, 84, 87
UNESCO *see* United Nations Educational, Scientific and Cultural Organization
United Nations 39–40, 42, 75, 78–9, 82–3, 114, 121–3, 133–42
United Nations Educational, Scientific and Cultural Organization 79, 82
United States 39, 42, 44, 58, 63, 101–9, 127–8
University of Central America 151
University of KwaZulu-Natal 22–30
University of St. Thomas 150, 154, 156–7
unknowability 43–4
unsettling common sense 7
"us vs them" mentality 88–9

Victims of Crime Survey 22–3
violent religious extremism 76, 79–80, 82, 90
Voltaire 56
vulnerability 152

Wajir Story, The 26
war crimes 48
War on Terror 69, 74, 89
war-mongering 22, 107

Ward, Thomas 85
ways of knowing 15
weapons of mass destruction 9
Weber, Max 69
Wehr, Paul 60
Weiler, Kathleen 139
Western educators 92–100
Western values 74, 76–7
what constitutes religion 68–72
Why I Became a Rebel 87
Wibben, Annick 4
Wieseltier, Leon 41
Wilson, Erin 69
winning a war 105–8
"wise sage on the stage" role 94
WMD *see* weapons of mass destruction
"Women of Burma Speak Out" 95
World Food Programme 135
World War II 1–7, 108

"youth bulge" 84

Zaradashti 116
zealotry 45
Zembylas, Michalinos 120
Zimbabwe 33–4
Zinn, Howard 101
"zone of peace" 138
Zwelethemba 26